GOD In Education

A New Opportunity for American Schools

GOD In Education
A New Opportunity for American Schools

by Niels C. Nielsen, Jr.

SHEED AND WARD: NEW YORK

© Sheed and Ward, Inc., 1966

Library of Congress Catalog Card Number 65-20860

Manufactured in the United States of America

Preface

This book has been written from the conviction that more attention should be given to the Supreme Court's suggestion concerning "teaching about religion." In refusing support for a constitutional amendment to reinstate Bible reading and prayers, the majority of Protestant leaders have recognized the larger problem of religion in education. Yet it is not at all clear that they have a relevant strategy. Roman Catholic attention continues to center on parochial institutions. One cannot be sure that the question of "teaching about religion" has been raised with sufficient clarity to allow either a positive or negative answer. Although the author is of Protestant background, no position has been accepted in this exposition simply because it is Protestant, Roman Catholic or Jewish!

Any effective strategy for strengthening religion in public education must be an ecumenical, indeed, an interfaith one. The new spirit of openness initiated by Pope John XXIII will inevitably have an effect on larger community relations. The author has served on consultative committees, both local and state, designed to help public school staffs understand their role in the face of changed conditions. It has been teachers and school administrators, as well as churchmen, who have

v

been caught between the extremes of sectarianism and secularism. This book offers no single answer, but is concerned with possible approaches which may open ways for a more positive expression of religious faith.

NIELS C. NIELSEN, JR.

Contents

	Preface	v
1	The Regents' Prayer Case and the Background of the Problem	3
2	Public Policy and the Separation of Church and State	13
3	Supreme Court Decisions and the Principles of Jefferson	25
4	The Crisis in Education	40
5	A Place for Religion in the Schools	55
6	Comparative Education: The Post-War German Experience	67
7	The Case for Christian Humanism	78
8	The Problem of Confessional Differences	93
9	Ecumenism and the Second Vatican Council	104
10	New Conditions and Common Problems	115
11	The French and German Traditions	127
12	The Parochial School and Religion in Higher Education	139

13 Teaching About Religion   153
14 The Non-Christian Religions   164
15 The Jewish View   175
16 Science and Religion   196
17 Communism and Religious Education   206
18 Prospects and Conclusions   228
    Index   241

GOD In Education
A New Opportunity for American Schools

1

The Regents' Prayer Case
and the Background of the Problem

The limits imposed on religion in public education by Supreme Court decisions continue to perplex both parents and teachers. Public attention centered most of all on the ruling against the so-called Regents' Prayer, which had been used voluntarily in some ten percent of the schools of the State of New York. The prayer was a short and completely non-denominational petition: "Almighty God, we acknowledge our dependence upon Thee, and we beg Thy blessings upon us, our parents, our teachers and our country." [1] Why should not school children be allowed to recite this prayer together, as long as those pupils who did not want to join in saying it could remain silent or be excused from the classroom? The legal ruling was that it violates the non-establishment clause of the First Amendment which has been made applicable to the states by the Fourteenth Amendment. The phraseology of the prayer was composed by public officials; government funds were used to support it as part of a public school program. In fact, the problem is not as simple as it first appears to be. Rejection of a single prayer would not have evoked such widespread public protest, the largest ever raised against any ruling by the Supreme Court. The Justices, like the public at large, knew that they were ruling on a much larger question: What recognition, if any, can be given in public education to faith in God?

The ruling against the Regents' Prayer was only one in a succession of Supreme Court decisions on the place of religion in state-supported schools. Whether or not one can agree with all that was said in the opinions handed down, one should not minimize the seriousness of the Justices' reflection. A year after it had ruled against the New York practice, the highest Court refused to give further legal sanction to Bible reading or the use of the Lord's Prayer. The public was not as surprised as by the Regents' Prayer decision. Yet there was widespread feeling in support of a constitutional amendment to give religion its "proper place." In rendering these important opinions, the Justices were more largely in agreement than in earlier decisions. Clearly, they were attempting to set a definite—in some respects a new—public policy. Bible reading had been supported by law in some states and rejected as illegal in others. The Supreme Court's position seems to be a simple one: Classroom prayers and Bible reading should not be conducted even when there is community consensus on religious questions. The public school is not a place for worship but for learning! Acts of religious devotion, by all the pupils in assembly, should be excluded from state-supported institutions. At the same time, the Supreme Court was most explicit that teaching about religion can be a legitimate part of secular instruction.

The demand for a constitutional amendment to allow Bible reading and prayers was at first strong. Congressional expressions of support for such a proposal were often outspoken, if not always explicit. That such an amendment

was not initiated after extensive legislative hearings does
not bespeak any desire for further secularization of education on the part of the American public. Responsible
church and school officials pointed out that long outstanding problems relating to religion in public education could
not be solved by constitutional amendment alone. The situation was assuredly not without humor. The bewilderment
of many citizens was expressed in the comic strip "Peanuts."
Charlie Brown and his small girl companion are shown
after they have returned home from school. She tells Charlie
of a deep secret which can be shared only in utmost confidence. The children look furtively through the house, peer
out the windows and at last take cover behind the sofa.
Finally, Charlie's friend tells him in a whisper, "We prayed
in school today." Another artist has portrayed a child kept
after class to write on the blackboard fifty times, "I will not
pray in school! I will not pray in school!" Still another car-
toonist has depicted a pupil remarking, before an examination, "It may be unconstitutional, but I am going to pray
anyhow."

What were the immediate issues at stake in the Regents'
Prayer case? Protest against the recitation of the prayer was
initiated by a New York businessman, Lawrence Roth, who
described himself as an unbeliever. Roth placed an adver-
tisement in local newspapers asking other parents to join
him in legal action. Four other families, all residents of the
small city of New Hyde Park, Long Island, just outside the
limits of Greater New York, agreed with him in challenging
the use of the Regents' Prayer. They charged that daily
recitation of the prayer was coercive, even when a pupil, on
parent's request, could step out of the classroom or remain
silent. Local authorities, defending use of the prayer, were
supported by the Board of Regents of the State of New York,
and sixteen parents of school children, Roman Catholic,
Protestant and Jewish. The Board of Regents, in sponsor-

ing the prayer, had been careful not to offend any major
religious group. Jewish opinion has long objected to whatever appears to be Christian usage in the public schools.
Roman Catholics have protested against Protestant Bible
reading, as in the State of Illinois, for example. More recently, Roman Catholic opinion has come to regard secularism more than Protestantism as the primary threat. The
lower courts had ruled that the prayer could be recited.
Judge Desmond of the New York Court of Appeals wrote
in support of this position:

> But it is not religious education nor is it the practice of or
> establishment of religion in any reasonable meaning of those
> phrases. Saying this simple prayer may be, according to the
> broadest possible dictionary, an act of religion, but when the
> Founding Fathers prohibited an establishment of religion they
> were referring to official adoption of or favor to, one or more
> sects. They could not have meant to prohibit mere professions of
> belief in God for, if that were so, they themselves in many ways
> were violating their rule when and after they adopted it.[2]

Did the prayer, with its starkly simple phraseology, really
violate the separation of church and state? The opinion
that it did not was supported by long-standing practice in
a variety of states. In Massachusetts, for example, there are
public schools which have begun their daily sessions with a
common act of devotion for over a hundred years. It is not
surprising that local and even state officials have been under
public pressure not to change existing practice. Some school
boards refused to comply with the Supreme Court ruling.
Were prayers before meals or on public occasions such as
graduation also to be abolished? The majority of parents and
teachers did not wish the further secularization of public
education. Yet the question remained: How is any significant
school religious observance possible in a society so drastically
pluralistic as that in the United States? The lowest common

denominator phraseology of the Regents' Prayer all too easily betrayed the abiding problem. Can children of Roman Catholics, Protestants, Jews and "unbelievers" engage in any more than token acts of devotion? The Supreme Court had "drawn a line" but had not necessarily brought the larger problem any closer to solution. *Commonweal* magazine commented:

What made the 1954 segregation decision particularly notable was its rich-textured awareness of the interplay between the constitutional rights and social responsibilities. By comparison, the prayer decision is crude, legalistic and naïve.[3]

Max Lerner wrote in the *New York Post* (June 27, 1962) :

I find too much absolutism in both Justice Black's and Justice Douglas' opinion. . . . They are both fearful that state intrusion into religion will cause religious discord in the society, yet the irony is that their decision has produced the most intense religious discord since the issue of Catholicism was raised in the 1960 campaign.[4]

Why did not more religious leaders make an all-out stand in defense of prayers and Bible reading? To be sure, strong statements were issued. Protestant opinion was divided; many clergymen urged more participation in home or church devotions. Roman Catholic interest often centered on the significance of the new rulings for parochial education. Fortunately, there was consideration as well for the difficulties faced in a judicial review of religious questions. The Supreme Court had attempted to draw some guidelines by setting minimum limitations in a briar patch of confusion. Historians and theologians rightly questioned part of what was said.[5] The Justices were not always in agreement with each other; they were not always consistent—so they had charged against each other in the earlier Zorach decision on released-time religious instruction. Old rules required redefinition and application in new circumstances. In the first of the series of rulings on religion and education, the Everson case, the Justices sought a minimum basis from which to proceed. Justice Black wrote:

The "establishment of religion" clause of the First Amendment means at least this: Neither a state nor the Federal Government can set up a church. Neither can pass laws which aid one religion, aid all religions, or prefer one religion against another. Neither can force nor influence a person to go to or to remain away from church against his will or force him to profess a belief or disbelief in any religion. No person can be punished for entertaining or professing religious beliefs, for church attendance or non-attendance. No tax, in any amount, large or small, can be levied to support any religious activities or institutions, whatever they may be called, or whatever form they may adopt to teach or practice religion. Neither a state nor the Federal Government can, openly or secretly, participate in the affairs of any religious organizations or groups and *vice versa*. In the words of Jefferson, the clause against establishment of religion by law was intended to erect "a wall of separation between church and state." [6]

In its later ruling against Bible reading and the Lord's Prayer, the Supreme Court was careful to hold that the state "may not establish a 'religion of secularism' in the sense of affirmatively opposing or showing hostility to religion. . . ." [7] Clearly, the Justices believe that the public school is not a religious but a civic institution, seeking to serve all citizens. It is not the primary agency in establishing religious attitudes in the community. In fact, it may reinforce some ideas and discourage others; basically, however, it is the churches and synagogues—Roman Catholic, Protestant and Jewish—which have the primary responsibility for the religious life of their constituencies. Justice Black, in hearing the second of the cases on religion in education (McCollum), insisted again that the state may not "aid all religions," a phrase which in fact means that it may not aid any religion. The paradox of the present educational situation is that the American people are in the majority actively religious. How deeply religious loyalties affect behavior can be debated, but certainly the prevailing ethos is not one of indifference. Justice Douglas wrote in his opinion on the Zorach case in 1952, "We are a religious people whose institutions presuppose a Supreme Being." The churches and synagogues are major community institutions; are their teachings to be completely without influence in public education?

A large number of public school teachers and administrators are persons of serious religious commitment. Many parents are concerned that the education of their children shall not be devoid of faith in God. They know as well that religion can contribute positively to character and moral development. On the other hand, there is the consideration that conscience cannot be compelled. More than this, confessional claims are potentially divisive. School administrators know from hard experience how easily religious conviction can lead to community tensions. They also know that if the Supreme Court rulings mean that the complaint of any parent who disavows religion is to be honored, little can ever be said or done positively. The question of disagreements between major religious parties is a different one. The first case in the present series of Supreme Court decisions on religion in education concerned bus transportation at public expense for pupils attending parochial schools. Justice Rutledge wrote, "This is not just a little case about bus rides." The Roman Catholic position, established in principle by papal encyclicals, is that religion and education belong together. It is important to understand that the conviction of many parents that their children shall not be trained in a context devoid of religious principles is as strong as, if not stronger than, that of those who wish the absolute exclusion of religion from public life.

Why has the question of the place of religion in government-supported education only recently reached the Supreme Court? One must remember that the public school system had not developed at the time of the writing of the Constitution. Education was largely under private auspices. Churches, which were in the main Protestant, were among its chief sponsors. The First Amendment applied only to the federal government. Support for religion in the several states continued into the early nineteenth century before being abolished in the face of a growing pluralism. The Fourteenth Amendment was passed after the Civil War to guarantee Negro rights. The legal background of the problem is not a complete explanation. Monsignor Joseph N. Moody, a careful Roman Catholic interpreter, points out that Protestantism more than secularism determined community attitudes.[8] Disagreement among its different denominations made for greater tolerance and freedom for other parties, Roman Catholic and Jewish. In fact, the structure of American society supported the Constitutional prohibition against establishment of religion.

Father William Kailer Dunn, in his doctoral dissertation at Johns Hopkins University, asked, "What happened to religious education?"[9] He concluded that the struggle over sectarianism, not hostility or indifference to religion, caused the decline of religious teaching in the public schools from 1825 until the Civil War. It was not believed that cooperation between church and state was unconstitutional, or that religion should not be encouraged by the state. Religion was acknowledged to have a legitimate place in public life; the First Amendment was not interpreted as driving a wedge between the church and society. In short, there was no purposeful expulsion of religious teaching in the sense of a divorce from culture. On the contrary, there was a fusion of secular and religious activities in governmental educational agencies. Nor was there a passing of authority from purely ecclesiastical or theocratic groups to state control. This change had already taken place.

Horace Mann is generally regarded as the "Father" of the public school in Massachusetts. Mann in fact established patterns which later spread throughout the nation. It is true that he worked effectively for the exclusion of Protestant sectarian teaching from the state-supported common school. He was explicit, however, in saying that there should be religious instruction to the fullest extent possible "without invading those rights of conscience which are established by the laws of God and guaranteed to us by the Constitution of the State." He wrote further, "Entirely to discard the inculcation of the great doctrines of morality and natural theology has a vehement tendency to drive mankind into opposite extremes; to make them devotees on the one side, or profligates on the other." [10] Father Neil G. McCluskey finds that this position was the only one which could have gained acceptance in the Massachusetts Commonwealth of the day.[11] The common truths of the Christian religion were to be taught in such a way that no particular sect would be favored. Mann opposed the teaching of doctrine and advocated instead a common-denominator approach to morality.

Nineteenth-century legislation and court decisions generally followed this tradition; sectarian religious instruction was forbidden in the public schools. Yet much that had specifically Christian roots remained. William T. Harris, the United States Commissioner of Education, advocated a more absolute separation of moral training from religion in the public school.[12] The school is to teach moral habits; the Church with its sacred surroundings and authoritative word is to communicate religious truth. To promote a non-sectarian religion, Harris argued, is really to establish one more sect. Although Harris proposed to exclude Bible reading from the classroom, he continued to presuppose a theistic consensus which can no longer be taken for granted today. It remained for modern pragmatism to reject fully the dualism of moral training and religious instruction. Dewey regarded democracy as a "spiritual community" which can overcome the dichotomy it poses by "regarding every child as a potential member of a democratic church." [13] This position has contributed to the contemporary ethos but has not resolved a continuing division of power and interest. The Supreme Court said little new when Justice Black wrote: "The First Amendment claims that both religion and government can best work to achieve their lofty aims if each is left free from the other *within its respective sphere*." [14] But what are the respective spheres of each? Does disestablishment mean the full separation of religion from education?

NOTES

1. Engle v. Vitale, 370 U.S. 421 (1962).
2. 10 N.Y. 2d 174; reprinted CR, July 2, 1962, p. 1152.
3. July 13, 1962.
4. Cited by Robert F. Drinan, *Religion, the Courts, and Public Policy* (New York: McGraw-Hill, 1963), p. 113.
5. Clyde A. Holbrook, "Religious Scholarship and the Court," *The Christian Century*, LXXX, 36 (September 4, 1963), pp. 1076–1078.
6. Everson v. Board of Education, 330 U.S. 1 at pp. 15–16.
7. Abington v. Schempp and Murray v. Curlett (June 17, 1963), Part V.
8. Joseph N. Moody, "A Catholic View of Contemporary Conflict," *The Outbursts That Await Us*, ed. Arthur Hertzberg (New York: Macmillan, 1963).
9. William Kailer Dunn, *What Happened to Religious Education? The Decline of Religious Teaching in the Public Elementary School* (Baltimore: Johns Hopkins Press, 1958).
10. Neil G. McCluskey, *Public Schools and Moral Education* (New York: Columbia University Press, 1958), p. 35.
11. Neil G. McCluskey, *Catholic Viewpoint on Education* (New York: Doubleday, 1962), p. 10.
12. *Ibid.*, pp. 42–45.
13. McCluskey, *Public Schools and Moral Education*, p. 266.
14. McCollum v. Board of Education, 333 U.S. 212 (1948).

2

Public Policy and
the Separation of Church and State

For more than a century and a half, the constitutional
prohibition against establishment of religion was not interpreted as a ban against Bible reading or prayer in the public
schools. Local control made possible a wide variety of practice. Many issues concerning the relation of religion and
education remained undecided. Not only have recent Supreme Court decisions attempted to establish greater uniformity; they have pointed up decisive issues. From 1791
to 1963, the Court ruled on less than a dozen major cases on
religion in public education.[1] Five cases, heard between 1947
and 1963, set new directions of policy. While the legitimacy of Bible reading and prayers has been taken for
granted as part of an accepted Protestant ethos, this consensus is now challenged. It is only recently that organized
groups within the American community have effectively
demanded its abandonment. The growing pluralism of religious life in the United States has been only one factor in
bringing about change. There has been rising secularist

pressure against any acknowledgment of belief in God in the public schools.

Some commentators have argued that belief in God is so deeply ingrained in American life that it will retain a place in education.[2] Litigation, they point out, cannot determine community attitudes. Only a major reversal of public opinion could remove it from the common life and practice. Yet one cannot overlook Justice Douglas' recent concurring opinion in which he advocated the thoroughgoing removal of religious influence and practice from all aspects of government. The Supreme Court decisions cannot by themselves alone determine the "wave of the future." To be sure, they mark an attempt to give direction to public policy and practice. Legal judgment rendered in a particular situation can set negative limits, but it cannot by itself bring about positive community relations. Father Drinan has written a discerning word of caution:

It is difficult to understand how much sound and fury could have been extended over these religious practices (prayer and Bible reading) . . . .

If the United States Supreme Court in one sweeping opinion forbade released or dismissed time, Bible-reading and the recitation of the Lord's Prayer, it seems unlikely that the basic nature or role of the public school in our society would be substantially changed. The elimination of all these practices would, of course, erect legal principles in Supreme Court jurisprudence which might well have an impact on the school curriculum of the next generation.[3]

The interpretation of the separation of church and state set forth by the Justices must be understood against the larger historical background of this doctrine, especially in the rejection of any form of established church. The religious traditions of the Founding Fathers were those of Enlightenment rationalism more than Reformation confessionalism. Basically they were not Jacobin, as in the French Revolution.[4] The men who held leadership in the new nation believed in God's existence, the moral law and immortality. Nominally they were more Protestant than Roman Catholic; in principle, they wished to avoid old confessional debates. Their faith was in Providence, reason and the values of tolerance. The documents of the American Revolution espoused a clear doctrine of natural law and viewed the struggle for independence as a defense of the rights of man. There was not the bitterness of Old World religious conflicts, too often expressed in anticlericalism. It was fortunate for the new nation that freedom of conscience as well as separation of church and state was established before the intense denominational feeling which developed in the nineteenth century. Religious pluralism, first among Protestant groups, then with Roman Catholics as well as "unbelievers," developed in new and unexplored patterns.

Dominant attitudes toward religion in education cannot be understood simply in terms of late eighteenth-century precedents. Institutional religion showed fresh vitality in the nineteenth century, by and large an era of great popular piety. Whereas active church membership was only 5 percent at the time of the American Revolution, it grew throughout the nineteenth century. A new religious interest on the frontier continued independently of Enlightenment rationalism and the ways of the older established denominations in the East. The Methodists, Baptists and Disciples of Christ recruited large numbers of adherents in the revivals. The nineteenth century was by and large a Protestant era in the United States. It was only after the Civil War that Irish, Italian, German and Polish Roman Catholic immigrants arrived in large enough numbers to constitute a significant sub-group. They not only developed an authentic American character, but were especially faithful in practice. The Jewish community, negligible in size at the time of the Revolution, also grew through immigration.

The Roman Catholic and Jewish communities are no longer made up primarily of immigrants. Instead, they have become part of the "established order," contributing in education as throughout national life to a new religious pluralism. Christianity can no longer be regarded as simply Protestant. The Jewish community, especially self-conscious in the face of Christian teaching, opposes any sectarian influence in public life. In addition, a fourth party has become more vocal. Its ultimate loyalty is secularist rather than theistic. The influence of this group is reflected in demands for the removal of all religion from public education. To be sure, the Roman Catholic and Jewish minorities have opposed what they have regarded as the remnants of Protestant religious practice in public education. For Roman Catholicism, at least, other issues are now at stake. The problem is no longer that of a predominately Protestant ethos but that of a positive role for religion in education under a variety of circumstances.

Commentators agree that public school life has now lost most of its Protestant religious character, in spite of the continued observance of such Christian holidays as Christmas and Easter. Prohibitions against sectarian religious instruction as part of a government-supported program of teaching have been written into law in many states. It is important to point out that the organizers of the first public schools did not intend that religion should have an exclusively Protestant character in public education. Of course, there was generally a working consensus of idea and belief among persons who assumed positions of leadership at the local level. Enlightenment faith was supplemented by Protestant piety without specific doctrinal teaching. In this sense, belief in God was not excluded. Reaction against the ethos of the public schools as too Protestant caused Roman Catholics to undertake their own parochial institutions under the leadership of the American hierarchy. The Bishops' Baltimore Declaration of 1884 required each parish to develop its own religious school as soon as possible. In time, the Roman Catholic Church in the United States became the sponsor of the world's largest parochial school system.

Some commentators describe the present controversy about the place of religion in public education as part of a larger struggle against ecclesiastical control.[5] To say the least, such appraisal oversimplifies complex historical circumstances and issues. The American public schools have been without ecclesiastical sponsorship virtually from the outset. There have been areas of agreement as well as disagreement between persons of different conviction in local communities. In fact, there has been a significant change of outlook in public education without a full, responsible appraisal of the religious implications of pluralism. Protestant moral instruction has long since been replaced by pragmatism as the dominant philosophy in public education. Although challenged on every side, pragmatism has not been modified to allow for a more lasting religious commitment. The reason is not difficult to find: It does not involve religious confessionalism or dogma. In the earlier, more optimistic period before the Second World War, it appeared to express the American belief in democracy. As the nation entered increasingly into competition with totalitarianism, it became clear that pragmatic compromise could give no justification for freedom or belief in the dignity of man. Recognition of the moral impotence of a view which discourages any ultimate faith commitments has led to larger concern for religion in education.

Can the religious parent allow his child to be educated in an environment which accepts none of his highest values? In a sense, all faith is sectarian to an agnosticism which

denies the possibility of religious knowledge. Dogmatic
secularist opinion has often overstated religious differences.
In fact there are common community ideals, many of which
are held with strong commitment. Jewish and Christian
parents feel responsibility to God for the moral and religious instruction of their children. Must the child who has
been taught religious faith in the home be completely silent
about it in the public school? The schoolroom determines
a large part of the child's attitude. It may reinforce or
negate the parents' judgment of what is of importance. How
far can the state go in insisting that all instruction be religiously neutral without establishing an essentially pagan environment? To be sure, there must be areas of compromise
as well as agreement between persons of different convictions in a pluralistic society. Yet is it fair to value religion
simply as sectarian or a private matter? The Supreme Court's
recent judgments—whether so intended or not—have seemed
to minimize the role of indigenous opinion and community
responsibility. They have taken questions of practice out of
local control, precluding discussion, compromise or cooperative action.

One need not be surprised that what appears to be an
attempt to restrict the place of religion in education has
prompted a reaction which transcends sectarian lines. Many
responsible citizens fear that the Supreme Court's position
may lead to the exclusion of religion from all of public
education. They believe that the democratic faith in the
dignity of man has some of its deepest roots in the Hebrew-
Christian tradition. Although no particular confession is
propagated by the state, responsibility to the moral law and
deity has been accepted in American public life. The Constitution, like the laws of the nation, was written in the conviction that there is a moral order in the universe. It does
not regard human government as the final authority or as
an end in itself. Education is not ethically neutral, but

inevitably premised on an interpretation of the meaning of human life. Decisions about values and character cannot be avoided in teaching; can such decisions be made in integrity without religious values? A system of education which is effective in denying all reference to an Absolute Good inevitably restricts the pupil's moral growth.

It is not in the American tradition that Jews should be asked to believe as Christians or Roman Catholics as Protestants. No one is to be compelled to prayer. The Constitution recognizes the right of every man to practice religion in accord with the dictates of his own conscience. It is important to note that the constitutional clause is a double one; it forbids any establishment of religion and at the same time safeguards the free exercise of religion. Of course, the chief purpose of public education is learning rather than worship. Devotion belongs particularly to the church, synagogue and home. The Protestant parent no less than the Roman Catholic does not wish to have his child compromise distinctive convictions in a lowest common denominator piety. He wishes to communicate the richness of his particular tradition to his children. The question is whether religious institutions can mediate their heritage completely isolated from the larger experience in education. Are all three major confessions to remain separated in a rigid communalism with cultural unity alone in a secular milieu? Of course, this may be necessary if the primary religious communities constitute "conspiracies against the common good," to use a phrase of John Courtney Murray.[6] If, on the contrary, our culture has historical roots and basic value convictions from the Hebrew-Christian tradition, an education which is cut off from it is impoverished.

Freedom of conscience in a democracy does not imply absolute separation of government from religious concerns. The Founding Fathers did not intend freedom *from* as much as freedom *for* religion! Church and state will have common

interests as long as faith remains vital and alive. For example, political leaders continue to call on the churches and
synagogues for help in support of international good will
and racial understanding as well as character-building activities. The Founding Fathers understood that both church
and state are corrupted when joined in a single power. But
they did not expect that religion should be driven out of
public life. Of course, religion is degraded when ecclesiastical appointments are made subject to political controversy
or public life is invaded by clericalism. Such practice does
not belong to the American tradition. Neither does the
claim that the state alone is supreme, self-sufficient and an
end in itself. Such absolute secularism is totalitarian rather
than democratic.

Responsible school officials and parents know that acknowledgment of belief in God does make a difference in
the ethos of the schoolroom. They ask why religion should
be restricted to private life or made a cause for embarrass-
ment in a nation whose pledge of allegiance to its flag includes the phrase "under God" and whose national anthem
carries the words "in God be our trust." Each time the
Supreme Court Justices convene in official session the clerk
intones the solemn phrase "God save the Court." Why must
the school day be begun differently? What a child is taught
about the meaning of life in the end does alter conduct. If
he understands that right and wrong are not just of his
own making, his life is set in a context of deeper meaning.
Ethical norms are understood as belonging to the structure
of the universe. A simply relativistic educational ethos, by
contrast, conveys the belief that man is his own beginning
and end. The exclusively secular appraisal of freedom which
espouses it as an end in itself needs careful re-examination.
The mere fact of choice does not assure responsible action.
If we expect students to be dedicated to liberty, they must
be taught respect for lasting norms which are more than

group mores or social conformity. The grounds of judgment are not simply emotional or subjective. All value positions are not equally valid.

Acknowledgment of a reality beyond the world and the human person provides the motivation for love of truth. Religious insight is crucial for the life of the child. Humility before God conditions not only conduct but the deepest personal loyalties. Knowledge is not oriented on pleasure; it is discovery more than invention. Life is not just what we choose to make of it; instead the moral law is obeyed or disobeyed. Neither the citizen nor his country is the last measure of righteousness or justice. Responsible teaching encourages the child to approach his own selfhood as other than a thing. Respect for persons is not a sectarian claim, established from the clash of one theory against another. It belongs rather to the common heritage of the Hebrew-Christian tradition, which teaches not only that persons are ethical beings, but that they are the creation of God. For Western man, this is not just one tradition among others. His attitudes and conduct are inexplicable apart from what it has taught concerning the dignity of the human person. To teach its primary values and meanings is not to make the school a church or synagogue, a place of salvation or of sectarian instruction.

The threat of religious communalism is assuredly the strongest argument in support of secularization. The Supreme Court's rulings may be regarded as an attempt to avoid a divisive confessionalism which will inevitably weaken education. Yet the question remains as to whether all religious influence is to be removed from public education. The legal structures of church-state relations in the United States were established from the Enlightenment conviction of tolerance—assuredly not in any anti-religious form. Creed and institutional church were minimized; individual liberty was given full range. Whatever the strengths and weaknesses of its sometimes deistic outlook, it did not deny the existence of God. This much is clear: The Founding Fathers did not envisage and would not have supported a thoroughgoing exclusion of all teaching about religion.[7] They were no more prepared to disavow questions of ultimate concern than to accept an unreflective dogmatic answer. Even their rationalism was concerned with essentially religious questions of the nature and destiny of man. The American public school system has developed in a way which they did not anticipate. Pluralism and a self-conscious secularism have brought the church-state question into new focus. The role of education itself has been revalued. Not merely a place for imparting information, the school has taken on a major role of community leadership.

Are the traditions of our national life flexible enough to adjust positively to the new pluralism? It would be naïve to suppose that questions of religion in public education can be resolved easily or without compromise. Good will is not enough; differences cannot be glossed over in a call to brotherhood, too often premised on indifference. Consensus is more difficult than before. Secularism is vocal in the argument that full exclusion of religion from public life is the only responsible alternative. Clearly the authors of the Constitution were not able to prophesy the nation's religious future. Roman Catholicism hardly came within their view as a possible major party. Judaism did not figure as an important factor in future controversy. In the face of changed conditions, would they favor only silence about of religion from public education? Whatever their judgment, they would be prepared to consider the issues in terms of the common welfare. It is clear that the dominant nineteenth-century pattern of sectarian, evangelical Protestantism is not to remain unchallenged. The new pluralism has come to stay.

One need not be surprised that many religionists still look

to the past, hoping to re-establish earlier patterns of dominance. Fortunately this attitude does not represent the majority of Protestant leadership. The spokesmen of the major denominations have recognized that there has been a break with an earlier Protestant culture. Marty has put the matter well: Americans formerly lived in a culture where the "wallpaper" was Protestant.[8] Clinging to the past, some refuse to believe that it must be changed; others find it only a bit faded. Most creative is the group which recognizes that a new wallpaper—a new context of life and work—is called for. Religious life has been enriched and at the same time become more pluralistic. One cannot expect indefinite retention of older cultural forms in changed conditions. The attempt to hold the ground for piety in the public school too easily reduces to a lowest common denominator. Why then should Christians continue to be concerned about the place of religion in education? Their interest can only lead to controversy! The issues at stake are easily oversimplified if appraised only in terms of the separation of church and state. A cultural tradition cannot be transmitted by the religious community alone. The school takes up so large a part of the student's time that no religious group can disregard its influence. Must religion in public education wait until religious groups have adjudicated all their differences? The issues are too pressing, the needs of public and parochial schools too immediate!

NOTES

1. Drinan, *Religion, the Courts, and Public Policy, op. cit.*, p. 3.
2. *Ibid.*, p. 7.
3. *Ibid.*, pp. 69–70.
4. Arthur Cohen, "The Problem of Pluralism," *Religion and the Free Society* (New York: Fund for the Republic, 1958), pp. 35–48.
5. This is in part Paul Blanshard's point of view in his *Religion and the Schools* (Boston: Beacon Press, 1963).

6. John Courtney Murray, "America's Four Conspiracies," in *Religion in America*, ed. John Cogley (Cleveland: World Publishing Company, Meridian Book, 1958), pp. 12–41.
7. Anson Phelps Stokes and Leo Pfeffer, *Church and State in the United States* (New York: Harper, 1964), pp. 30f.
8. Martin E. Marty, "The Protestant Reinterpretation of American Life," in *The Outbursts That Await Us,* ed. Arthur Hertzberg (New York: Macmillan, 1963).

3

Supreme Court Decisions
and the Principles of Jefferson

The principles affirmed in the series of cases which began with a favorable Supreme Court ruling on bus transportation subsidy for parochial schools, and ended with a ban on prayer and Bible reading, cannot really be set forth simply in terms of generalities. They must be traced out step by step as they developed in consecutive decisions. In the Everson case, the Justices ruled that a grant from tax funds for bus transportation to parochial schools was legal as pupil aid. The decision also included Justice Black's statement that, "Neither a state nor the Federal Government can . . . pass laws which aid one religion, aid all religions, or prefer one religion over another." The principles set forth in this ruling were cited by attorneys arguing against released-time religious instruction in the public schools. Summarizing their case against the practice, they concluded:

It seems . . . that without any hesitancy it can be said that unless this Court is now prepared to delete from the opinions

25

in that case the strong language that was used, unless it is prepared to renounce the principles set out by the majority—and, so far as that is concerned, concurred in by the minority—then the decision in this case must be necessarily in favor of the appellant.[1]

The released-time program began as an attempt to develop major religious education apart from the Sunday School or parochial institutions and was first employed in Indiana in 1913. Each child was released by his public school for religious instruction during school hours with parental consent. After such consent had been given, attendance was compulsory. The parents of Terry McCollum brought legal action against released-time instruction in the public schools of Champaign, Illinois, on the grounds that it violated the First Amendment of the Constitution. Religious teaching took place in the school buildings; the cost to the school board was negligible. The Supreme Court ruled the practice unconstitutional, in part on the grounds of cost to the state, and Justice Frankfurter wrote:

We renew our conviction that "we have staked the very existence of our country on the faith that the complete separation between the state and religion is best for the state and best for religion." If nowhere else, in the relation of Church and State, "good fences make good neighbors." [2]

An important new precedent was established in the McCollum decision. The Supreme Court denied that "the purpose of the 'establishment' clause was only to insure protection for the 'free exercise of religion.' " For the first time in American jurisprudence, a plaintiff was allowed to invoke the First Amendment against a practice which aids religion without any infringement of his own rights. The Supreme Court departed from earlier practice by interpreting the establishment clause alone, apart from the free exercise clause. Justice Stewart challenged this view in his dissent in the Regents' Prayer case: "the Court does not hold, nor could it, that New York has interfered with the free exercise of anybody's religion." [3] Formerly, a person complaining was required to show that there was some restriction on his religious freedom. With the McCollum case, the mere presence of a violation of the establishment clause created in the non-believer a right to have a particular practice enjoined. On this interpretation, the First Amendment prescription against establishment is not simply a means by which religious freedom is secured for all. It gives the non-believer the right to have all aid to religion enjoined. On this ground, the Regents' Prayer could be ruled unconstitutional.

The McCollum judgment evoked widespread public protest. More than a million and a half pupils were enrolled in released-time programs across the nation, in an attempt to supplement secular public school instruction with religious training. In a second decision on this type of arrangement, the Supreme Court accepted a New York plan which used private buildings, primarily church units. It held that the separation of church and state need not be absolute in released-time instruction. A number of commentators protested that most of what McCollum had done was undone! [4]

The Court justified its approval of released-time instruction on the grounds that no use of public school classrooms or expenditure of state funds was involved. Actually, as we have noted, the expenditure of government money in Illinois had been minimal. The Supreme Court's second statement on released-time religious instruction showed larger appreciation for the subtleties of church-state relations. Again, there was not complete agreement among the judges. The three Supreme Court Justices who opposed the New York plan argued, in dissent, that the later Zorach decision misconstrued the earlier McCollum ruling. Nonetheless, the majority of the Court concluded that the "First Amendment does not say that in every and all respects there shall be a separation of Church and State." Instead, its primary proscription is directed against any "concern or union or dependency one on the other."

The "wall of separation" metaphor was not used. Justice Douglas' later support for full secularization had not yet developed. If the law in question were to be condemned as unconstitutional, he noted, a variety of other practices must also be declared in violation of the First Amendment:

Churches could not be required to pay even property taxes. Municipalities would not be permitted to render police or fire protection to religious groups. Policemen who helped parishioners into their places of worship would violate the Constitution. Prayers in our legislative halls; the appeals to the Almighty in the messages of the Chief Executive; the proclamations making Thanksgiving Day a holiday; "so help me God" in our courtroom oaths—these and other references to the Almighty that run through our laws, our public rituals, our ceremonies—would be flouting the First Amendment.[5]

However, the Supreme Court strictures against aid for nonpublic church-related schools were reaffirmed. Government "may not finance religious groups . . . nor blend secular or sectarian instruction."

In fact, institutional religion receives large subsidy in the form of tax exemption. No court in the United States has ever ruled against this special privilege as discriminatory toward unbelievers, although it is challenged by the parties which secured the abolition of school prayers. A ruling against such tax exemption would have major institutional consequences. However, as recently as April 1962, the Supreme Court refused to review a case from Rhode Island in which present practice was challenged. In addition to this tax exemption, federal government expenditure totals more than one hundred million dollars annually for chaplains in the armed forces. Such use of government funds is recognized by the courts on the grounds that it supports the free exercise of religion for persons who have been taken away from the usual community resources. Still more direct subsidy to institutional religion is given in the form of substantial government grants to Protestant, Roman Catholic and Jewish social agencies. All major Protestant denominations have accepted subsidy under the Hill-Burton Hospital Construction Act which was passed in 1946. The legislation authorized the federal government to pay from one-third to two-thirds of the cost of buildings and equipment within designated areas of need. Any private "non-profit" group is eligible to receive federal funds after approval of its medical standards by the state department of health. In his concurring opinion in the Regents' Prayer Case, Justice Douglas observed with dismay that the whole structure of government is "honeycombed" with expenditures of state funds for purposes with which religion is intermingled.

There can be little doubt that the Supreme Court will be called on to act as arbiter in the future as controversy about the role of religion in education continues. Arthur Cohen describes the situation as follows:

The Supreme Court is confronted with the unenviable task of defining law in matters affecting religion and government. It has at its disposal a regrettably limited, tersely expressed, and by no means unambiguous set of legal categories, for those provided by the First and Fourteenth Amendments supply but limited direction. Every decision the Justices have formulated in the past fifteen years has been read by some as a shameful concession to organized religion, and by others as a further reinforcement of the total secularization of our culture. The result has been that some disputants were dissatisfied, clarity was only momentarily achieved, and our jurists remained doomed to await another opportunity to rethink positions and decide again. This, of course, is how the law grows. But it is also the means by which the people's lack of clarity is perpetuated and their refusal to accept responsibility deepened.[6]

For the first time in the history of the United States, major federal funds have been commited in support of elementary and secondary schools. A national educational policy is developing as the federal government supplies resources not available at the state or local levels. Religious controversy had been a factor in delaying federal aid bills in the Eisenhower and Kennedy administrations. Relatively swift congressional approval of President Johnson's program, proposed early in 1965, showed that some limited consensus about national needs as well as possible strategies had been achieved. The Johnson program was premised on the view that public welfare benefits for church-sponsored education are constitutional; direct subsidy but not indirect aid has been excluded by Supreme Court decisions. The larger part of the new national appropriation is designated for state-directed education. However, limited help for non-profit private schools, primarily Roman Catholic parochial institutions, has also been included.

The "poverty impact" program called for in Title I of the "Elementary and Secondary Education Act of 1965" carries the largest subsidy. Technically, this part of the new legislation is an amendment to an earlier 1950 statute. It provides federal funds to redress "the impact that concentrations of low income families have on the ability of local educational agencies to support adequate programs. . . ." The local agency filing an application must establish

that, to the extent consistent with the number of educationally deprived children in the school district of the local educational agency who are enrolled in *private elementary and secondary* schools, such agency has made provision for including special educational services and arrangements (such as dual enrollment, educational radio and television, and mobile educational services and equipment) in which such children can participate. . . .

Funds under this part of the act are made available directly only to public school agencies; however, the latter have explicit responsibility to provide that dual enrollment or some other appropriate arrangement be available for educationally deprived children who are attending non-public schools. In some circumstances, the new resources may be limited to "mobile educational services" for handicapped children unable to attend school. It is generally conceded, however, that more extensive shared-time programs will be expected and required.

The shared-time program is assuredly one of the most creative proposals yet offered to help solve the public-parochial school dilemma. Largely Protestant initiated, it nonetheless has attracted widespread Roman Catholic interest. A most widely discussed formulation was proposed by a Presbyterian layman, Harry J. Stearns, the Superintendent of Schools in Englewood, New Jersey.[7] Prior to the new national legislation, the United States Commissioner of Education, Francis Keppel, recommended shared time to a House of Representatives subcommittee as a necessary part of a general school aid bill. Even before federal support, the plan was being tried out in many different communities across the nation. Students take part of their classes in the parochial school; other instruction, particularly in the sciences, is given in the public school. The pupil's day is thus shared. The cost of parochial education is reduced. All children in the community have at least part of their day in common.

Superintendent Stearns supports his shared-time proposal with the following arguments: First, it recognizes the freedom and right of parents to direct the education of their

children. Secondly, it respects the claims of those religious
parties which hold that the child's education cannot be
rightfully determined by the state alone; the child belongs
to God and not just to the nation. Thirdly, shared time
envisages pluralism rather than a single conformist position
in education. It would not violate the Supreme Court's
ruling that religious instruction cannot take place in public
school buildings, but only in private facilities. However,
shared time is broader in scope than the released-time practices reviewed by the Court in the McCollum and Zorach
cases. It reaches into a much larger part of the pupil's school
time. In view of the differences between these decisions, it
is not fully clear how the Supreme Court will rule on it.

Theodore Powell, Public Information Consultant of the
State Department of Education in Hartford, Connecticut—a
state where shared time has been practiced for some time—
has written of the constitutional question:

The principles enunciated in the Louisiana textbook (Cochran) case and the New Jersey School Bus (Everson) case by the
Supreme Court provide a constitutional basis for shared time
programs.

There are three essential points:

1. The service or instruction must have a public purpose, not
a religious purpose.

2. Conversely, the expenditure of public funds and the public
service must be under public control.

3. The service or instruction must be available to all pupils
of the same category (that is, there must not be arbitrary or
unreasonable discrimination) .[8]

Paul Blanshard has commented:

There is nothing specific in the First Amendment or in the
Supreme Court cases about that amendment to exclude the
idea of attendance of parochial students at public schools on a

part-time basis. They are American children, entitled under the law to enroll at any public school. The real questions concerning constitutionality arise when the details of administration and practice are considered. . . . The Court might declare the arrangement unconstitutional under the theory championed by Justice Frankfurter in his concurring opinion in the McCollum case that there is a "requirement to abstain from fusing functions of Government and of religious sects." [9]

The new legislation is of limited scope. It requires only that dual enrollment be available to underprivileged pupils for whom the federal government provides subsidy. Moreover, from the Roman Catholic point of view, shared time is less than ideal. Division of a pupil's day threatens to break down the organic wholeness of his education. In spite of this limitation, there has been serious Roman Catholic consideration of the plan in view of present needs. Clearly, experiment is necessary to the development of programs. The shared-time proposal seems easier to implement at the junior and senior high school levels than the lower grades. A major practical problem is one of scheduling; teacher as well as pupil time must be arranged. There is general agreement among school administrators that lines of jurisdiction must be carefully delimited between public and parochial schools, in order to guard against possible conflicts of interest. Shared time needs to be presented in such a way that the entire community understands what is being undertaken. Court review must inevitably consider what has taken place at the local level.

Title II of the "Elementary and Secondary Education Act of 1965" provides textbook and library subsidy for parochial as well as public schools. State educational agencies are to apply for grants, and to include non-public schools in their request. Where state law forbids such cooperation between public school agencies and church-sponsored schools, the Office of the United States Commissioner of Education is to provide such materials on an equitable basis. The materials are to be the same in public and private schools and cannot be used for sectarian instruction or religious worship. The legal precedent for the constitutionality of such enactment is the 1930 Supreme Court decision in the case of Cochran v. Louisiana State Board of Education. The Court unanimously sustained a Louisiana statute which provided for the state loan of textbooks to both public and parochial schools.

Title III of the new legislation calls for federal sponsorship of a variety of educational services and centers. Among the activities included under this part of the act are guidance, remedial instruction, specialized instruction and equipment for handicapped or pre-school children and students in advanced scientific subjects and foreign languages, special educational services for persons in rural areas, assistance to adult education, and production of radio and television programs for educational use. A grant for supplementary educational services may be made to a local educational agency "only if there is satisfactory assurance that in the planning of that program there has been, and in the establishing and carrying out of that program there will be, participation of persons broadly representative of the cultural and educational resources of the area to be served." Such resources include "State educational agencies, institutions of higher education, non-profit private schools." Title IV amends the Cooperative Research Act of 1954, granting funds to universities, colleges and other public and private non-profit agencies as well as to individuals for research in the field of education. Title V provides for the strengthening of state departments of education.

There can be little doubt that President Johnson's proposal was a compromise. He and his advisors chose the strategies least likely to be challenged as unconstitutional. Public money is not to be spent to aid religion, but only to protect the health and welfare of children. The constitutional question with respect to the new legislation is how far public welfare benefits can be extended. New precedents are being established in the range and scope of the program, and these will be subject to court review. What Dean Drinan has written of shared time, may well extend to all parts of the new program:

Shared-time could cause Catholics to have more interest in the public school with the result that their voting power in various communities might be a factor in the improvement of the financial condition of public schools. Finally, it might be useful in bringing together *all* of the children of a community for part of their education and by this means promote a greater solidarity among all future citizens.[10]

Arthur Cohen stresses that the Zorach decision showed a willingness by the Supreme Court to acknowledge that no formulation with regard to either separation or establishment can be fully final.[11] He emphasizes that the Court must and will continue to redefine its understanding in response to the unfolding of events and the exigencies of history. Increasingly, tension-ladened situations will develop if such proposals as shared time remain completely unimplemented. It would be tragic if the strongly competitive character of religious life in the United States as well as outspoken secular pressure should cripple experiment with such tentative solutions. The intrinsic limitations of such programs as shared time make evident common problems which cannot be resolved exclusively by any single religious body. It is in the American tradition of pluralism that a solution should be sought by voluntary cooperation of different community agencies, rather than from a centralized authority alone. To be sure, national educational policy ought not to be circumscribed by the special interests or confessional claims of any party. Yet, one must ask whether such a policy can be effective if church-sponsored

institutions are excluded completely from federal programs
for upgrading education.

It was Thomas Jefferson who wrote of "building a wall of
separation between Church and State." A number of recent
studies have attempted to appraise his attitude toward present issues. Although history does not tell us what he would
say today, his past statements nevertheless remain a matter
of record. In his definitive study on Church and State
in the United States, Anson Phelps Stokes cites the fact
that Jefferson ordered works on the evidences of Christianity for the library at the University of Virginia.[12] Stokes
concludes: "Even in establishing a quasi-state university on
broad lines, the greatest liberal who took part in founding
our government felt that instruction in the fundamentals
of Christian theism and Christian worship were both important and proper." Stokes argues that Jefferson shared
the double interest common to most of the Founding
Fathers. He supported religion because he was himself religious and believed that without religion democracy could
not succeed. He wished to insure religious freedom by doing away with any form of government interference in religious matters.

Did Jefferson favor a completely secular school? What was
the relation between his conviction that the church and
state should be separate and his support of public education? In his *Jefferson on Public Education,* Robert M.
Healey argues that the connection between the two is often
exaggerated. "Nor can his [Jefferson's] understanding of the
proper role of religion in public education be seen rightly
as a development of his concept of the doctrine of separation
of church and state." [13] According to Healey, Jefferson did
not ask: How does the First Amendment govern what is
possible in the field of religion? Instead, he accepted the
Amendment as a given condition of democratic life in the

Republic. His question was rather, what can be done to provide the fullest instruction in all useful sciences, of which religion is the most important? In support of this view, Healey cites the plans which Jefferson helped to draw up for the new University of Virginia.

Jefferson explicitly expressed faith in God as creator, pre-server, regulator and supreme judge, as well as in personal immortality. Uninterested in abstract metaphysical specula-tion, he based his position on characteristic Enlightenment premises—reason, nature and man's innate moral sense. His own search for truth was expressed in his letter to Peter Carr:

Religion. Your reason is now mature enough to examine this object. In the first place, divest yourself of all bias in favor of novelty and singularity of opinion. Indulge them in any other subject rather than that of religion. It is too important, and the consequences of error may be too serious.[14]

Jefferson accepted the argument for cause-effect and design as conclusive. He attached most importance to the general consensus about God's existence. His letter to John Adams on April 11, 1823, included the following:

So irresistible are those evidences of an intelligent and powerful Agent that, of the infinite numbers of men who have existed through all time, they have believed in the proportion of a million at least to Unit, in the hypothesis of an eternal pre-existence of a creator, rather than in that of a self-existent Universe. Surely this unanimous sentiment renders this more probable than that of the few in other hypothesis.[15]

Jefferson's search for religious truth was integrated with his belief in democracy. He found that state encroachment on freedom of religion had not ended with the coming of Christianity. Instead, it continued in established religious institutions in Europe even to his lifetime. Although Jefferson appraised religion primarily from the moral point of view, his protest was in the name of truth and not indifference. He believed that Jesus taught morality in its highest form and reacted most keenly against those who abused it in the name of religion. Education should lead the student to believe in the benevolence of God. Increased maturity brings growing appreciation of the rational arguments for the "being of a God, the creator, preserver, and supreme ruler of the universe." [16] Jefferson believed that if all points of view were allowed to be heard, reason in the end would triumph. Such discussion belonged to public education as much as to private schools. It should take place most of all in the universities. However, religion is necessary to education at all levels, as it makes men moral.

Jefferson opposed the Virginia clergy, especially the Presbyterians, and insisted that they should be excluded from the legislature as well as from educational appointments. He would no more allow their dominance in politics than he would countenance state interference in religious matters. Government, while still supporting religion as essential to democracy, has no right or power to control its primary convictions. Jefferson expected different points of view and conflict in the community. Healey speculates that he believed that primitive Christianity, as he understood it, would soon take hold throughout the land.[17] In this, Jefferson was mistaken; revivalism displaced Enlightenment intellectualism. It can hardly be denied that he oversimplified the issue of religion in public education by limiting teaching to moral principles and arguments for the existence of God.

On first examination, Jefferson's position is clear enough. He believed that religion should be included in the public school curriculum in areas where there is common agreement in the community. Questions on which there is disagreement should be left to the different sects themselves. His position, in fact, requires mutually recognized and defined agreement and disagreement in the community. The common conviction necessary to a democracy will not come from enforced secularization, but from voluntary deliberation, trust and mutual understanding. It is clear that even in the presence of disagreement, Jefferson would not propose to eliminate all religion from education because it is controversial. Instead, he would continue to insist that it is fundamental in the training of democratic citizens. Yet he did not tell us what to do when community consensus breaks down.

NOTES

1. Record of oral arguments in McCollum v. Board of Education, p. 60.
2. McCollum v. Board of Education, 333 U.S. 232 (1948), cited from Everson v. Board of Education, 330.
3. Engel v. Vitale, 370 U.S. 445 (1962).
4. Including some members of the Supreme Court, in dissent from the majority.
5. Zorach v. Clauson, 343, U.S. (1952).
6. Cohen, *op. cit.*, 41.
7. Harry L. Stearns, "Shared Time: A Proposal for the Education of Children," *Religious Education* (January-February 1962), pp. 5–10.
8. Theodore Powell, "Shared Time in Hartford," *Religious Education* (January-February 1962), p. 36.
9. Blanshard, *op. cit.*, p. 180.
10. Drinan, *op. cit.*, p. 161.
11. Cohen, *op. cit.*
12. Stokes and Pfeffer, *op. cit.*, 1950 ed., pp. 338–339, 515–516.
13. Robert M. Healey, *Jefferson on Public Education* (New Haven: Yale University Press, 1962), pp. 11–14.
14. *Ibid.*, pp. 23–24.
15. *Ibid.*, p. 28.
16. *Ibid.*, p. 27.
17. *Ibid.*, p. 205.

4

The Crisis in Education

Public education in the United States is undergoing drastic reappraisal in virtually every area. It is commonplace to point to the advent of the Russian Sputnik as the turning point which aroused American public opinion. Curricula and methods of instruction are in transition, and it is not fully clear what character they will take in the future. This much is certain: The roots of the crisis go deeper than any recent technological development. An alleged equalitarianism has led to a relaxation of standards. Every child must be encouraged equally! This notion has been supported by a utopian hope that the democratic ideal would remake not only the individual but society itself. Pragmatic compromise would lead to a new way of life. A swift sequence of events in the last decade has called this educational outlook into question. A new self-consciousness in the face of competition with other nations, especially the Russians, has brought increased pressure for excellence. Is education really "effective" in our culture? Public opinion has demanded that it be equal to the best in any country! There has been an upgrading of subject matter not only in the sciences but in the humanities as well.

The difficulties of educating for the future—in the face of rapidly changing national and international circumstances—should not be oversimplified. Who can say what changes will come about even in our present lifetimes? Yet ignorance at this point is no excuse for neglecting present urgent needs. The sheer magnitude of the immediate educational problem—from the neglected urban school to expanding university research—defies any simple solution. Approximately one fifth of the total population spends the principal part of its day in the classroom. The wave of war babies, which has already overtaxed facilities at the lower levels, is now reaching college. More than this, an ever-increasing percentage of the citizenry continues in specialized training beyond high school, through four years of college, into graduate school. School plants are inadequate and teaching often does not bring maximum results at the lower grades. It is estimated that the demand for increased facilities and staff will require at the very least the doubling of existing facilities in colleges and universities in coming decades.

What are the circumstances which have put so high a priority on the need for trained persons? We need not look far for an answer. Atomic energy and intercontinental missiles have dramatized the importance of science. Congress has given large federal support not only to the space program, but to a wide diversity of scientific studies and research. The impact of this strategy is now being felt in high school instruction. A maximum of ingenuity and imagination has been called into play in teaching science and related subjects such as mathematics. New teaching methods have been worked out with the help of the National Science Foundation, an agency supported by federal government grants. Foreign languages are receiving similar encouragement. The need for increased content as well as for national standards has been emphasized by a variety of critics. Modern nations engage in "total competition" in education. Technology does not stand alone. National defense requires that we ask what is being done with all of our educational resources. The specially talented pupil must not be held back by less creative fellow students. Knowledge and character need to develop together.

The trend toward increased factual knowledge in history and literature as well as science—as against life-adjustment or group-living programs—is probably not to be arrested. There is an increasing conviction in public discussion that the school is first of all a place to learn. Responsible measurement of achievement is being demanded at every level. Depressed urban situations which breed indolence and delinquency must be upgraded. The problem of developing a responsible citizenry is of increasing difficulty in large cities where there is not equal opportunity for persons of different economic and racial backgrounds. The total complex of social circumstances does not bring forth the maximum learning potential or allow for the fullest creative growth. Dr. James B. Conant, former president of Harvard, among others, has pointed out in careful studies how much needs to be undone, how much more to be reconstructed, if our society is to meet the demands which the future places upon it.[1] Firm standards must be maintained at every level. The underprivileged need to be given a fair opportunity. It would be a mistake to suppose that the American experiment has been a failure in education. Yet false pride and rationalization can be of no real help in the present circumstances.

Max Lerner, author of *America as a Civilization,* has appraised its achievement with fine insight:

The American public-school system, created by this educational revolution in New England and followed later by a revolution of higher education in the Land-Grant Colleges of the Middlewest, helped create a remarkable degree of cohesiveness in a polyglot America composed of varied ethnic, regional and religious groups.[2]

The first revolution in the American educational experiment prepared Americans for life as citizens in a democratic republic.

It helped create a nation as a going concern with an impressive capacity for building a prosperous economy, a tolerably open society, a reasonably effective government of laws and men. . . .[3]

As a sociologist, Lerner reports that American civilization now shows the weakness of any mass society—mediocrity, sloppiness and the cult of barren method.

The achievements of the past must be appropriated creatively if knowledge is to be advanced and new problems faced with insight. This is perhaps most difficult in a democracy where education is so dependent on public support. It is the responsibility of teaching to convey a total cultural heritage. Yet schools inevitably reflect the resources and values of the society in which they function. Of course, it is to be hoped that from time to time they may share a wider outlook which sees beyond immediate needs. Community as well as professional leadership earlier supported the so-called progressive educational movement, the major theoretical expression of the period. Now unpopular, it assuredly receives the blame for more evils than it deserves. Nonetheless, its decline is a recognized fact of the American educational scene. Against its critics, its advocates have offered suprisingly little defense in recent years. Cremin argues that it first lost its intellectual creativity and then became a tradition without roots.[4] Public education in the United States has been directed by a complex of forces—business, political and scientific. The optimistic, progressivistic outlook which prevailed from the turn of the century until the era of the Second World War reflected the dominant cultural ethos—its utopian belief in success as well as its scientism. Dewey's naturalism was only one expression of a faith which has been called into question in the face of new ideological and power challenges to our civilization.

In short, there is a crisis in the need for expanded facilities and the upgrading of teaching. There is as well a moral crisis as to the meaning of education itself and the values it should exemplify. It would be a mistake to suppose that education in the United States can or will return to a classically simple curriculum. The demands of modern life, in particular an increased emphasis on scientific change, preclude so simple a solution. Although the culture in which progressive education flourished has changed drastically with the advent of two world wars, an important legacy remains. Dr. Conant has summarized its contribution in terms of new teaching methods: earlier patterns of instruction had broken down.[5] A school revolution which began in Massachusetts was carried nation-wide by Dewey and his followers. Its goal was to make the classroom, especially at the elementary level, more humane as well as more interesting. In the high school, a greatly increased range of curriculum came into being with the initiation of the elective system. Both developments might have come about without progressive education. Actually, the new philosophy emphasized well their importance. Cremin points out that the coalition of business, political and scientific leadership which supported change has now broken down.[6] The private schools which once encouraged progressive education now direct attention to maximum content in preparation for college.

The general lowering of standards in accommodation to popular demand cannot be blamed entirely on progressive education. Dewey himself did not support such compromise, but argued instead that the schools should upgrade public life.[7] Myron Lieberman in his study *The Future of Public*

Education comments incisively on the deterioration of curriculum and teaching procedures: local control has imposed unreasonable limits on school leadership. Academic accomplishment has been seriously downgraded in response to the demand that all persons in the community must be happy and controversy avoided![8] Democratic control has too often meant conformity to generally accepted standards of mediocrity! The integrity of teaching inevitably suffers under such circumstances. Lieberman argues that the ineffectiveness of public education cannot be remedied apart from new freedom and professional status for teachers. With respect to students, it must be recognized that there are marked differences in ability. Equalitarian practice in which all children are regarded as of equal potential has been challenged by practical necessities of scientific training. How is this fact to be dealt with in view of the democratic commitment to the education of all citizens? Max Lerner writes:

> The two answers locked in conflict today are roughly those of discipline and love. . . . But neither of these is the direction in which we can aim at the jugular in education. Given the ills and vulnerabilities of a mass society, the first great task of education is to develop a sense of the core of identity in oneself and of the authentic in whatever one's life touches.[9]

Lerner emphasizes that education must develop persons who are more than interchangeable units of a mass. It must seek to shape a creative culture within the mass society and even out of many materials. Only a small part of a society can be expected to show real creativeness; authenticity need not be so limited.

In the United States, the common school has been an assimilative agency which has transcended particular national backgrounds. Far more than in other cultures, it has built bridges of understanding between persons of different views. As an institution with diversified activities, it has at

times taken over "socialization" and "life-adjustment," functions reserved to the family or even the church in other
cultures. The pragmatic ethos of progressive education,
quite apart from any self-conscious presuppositions, has
shown little concern for the True or even for the Good.
Abiding knowledge and norms have been minimized together. Those who oppose such anti-intellectualism have
found that the task of refuting it is little short of monumental. It can be overcome educationally only by participation in a tradition whose questions and meanings have
been nearly lost to both teachers and students. They have
been taught to view all "practically"—including religion.
In spite of its derogation of metaphysics, such an outlook
does have its own view of reality with an accompanying
appraisal of man and his status in the world. That which is
normative belongs with adjustment, the relative and practical! Actually, the danger of such a premise is that it will
produce a sub-ethical community which really does value
only the survival of the "fittest."

The pragmatic compromises on which so much of educational theory has been based are now called into question
by new circumstances. The basic values to which American
education is dedicated are no longer regarded as self-evident; the consensus about them is in question. In fact, they
have not been so much experimental and scientific as faith
premises. They are part of a larger judgment about the
meaning of life as well as the goals and ends to which our
society is committed. Against an abstract idealism, pragmatism has rightly emphasized that effective value patterns
are not taken from the air "full blown." They grow out of
needs and circumstances, the ambitions and hopes of particular people. However, pragmatism has not made clear
enough that science alone cannot give life values, much
less tell man what he ought to be. Robbed of its naïve
hopefulness, scientism really leads to amorality and nihi-

lism. Modern technology has been employed by totalitarian states as well as by democracies for their respective ends. Questions of abiding meaning and value press in on democratic society in the face of its belief in the dignity of man. The traditional resources for supporting such belief have been in large measure religious. Are religious resources now to be denied as controversial and "sectarian" in public education?

Bereft of progressivistic inspiration, educational procedure now seeks strength and rigor in technology. But the vacuum of goals remains. The pupil is to know—what to do or be? By what norms shall he choose or act? Is there to be respect for truth which transcends the useful? Naïve democratic equalitarianism is rejected. The student is to be trained more rigorously than before. Competition in the lower grades as well as for entrance to college and university raises standards. Yet the confusion in values is not resolved. A democratic society is to be an open one, but what is to to be its working unity or consensus: the relativity of truth? Only the factual belongs in the curriculum; other concerns for reality are controversial and to be avoided! But are facts self-evident or known apart from values or interpretation? What is at stake in the world competition in education? Would American science really have been effective in the Second World War if it had not been supported by a considerable number of outstanding refugees from Europe? The Russians, too, have made remarkable progress in technological "know-how." Does such "know-how" guarantee respect for the dignity of the human person? Shall the larger cultural tradition from which science grew be abandoned or re-affirmed in new sensitivity?

Max Lerner has pointed out that there are two great systems of education expanding all over the globe. The Russian initiative is in support of Communism. The American effort, both governmental and private through foundation aid, seeks a larger freedom for the individual. Lerner, although appreciative of past achievements, warns that the task of American culture in the future is not as easy as may appear in oversimplified analysis:

> The second revolution has a double task. The first is to counteract the hollow homogenizing tendencies of a mass society, in which so much happens that does not authentically belong to the experience of living, feeling, and thinking, but is pseudoliving, synthetic feeling and derivative thinking. . . . The individual, instead of becoming a person, is thus in danger of becoming merely an interchangeable unit of a mass. . . .[10]

Lerner proposes a transvaluation of values in education:

> Instead of the three R's I suggest that the new imperatives of our time are the Three Knows: to know your world and your civilization and the forces that have shaped it and are reshaping it; to know your craft, whatever it may be and to know it with precision and with passion; to know yourself, to make that Journey into the Interior which is the most difficult journey anyone is ever called upon to make.[11]

The teacher is to belong to the elite, not from privilege but from creativity. Instead of success, value is to be put on the capacity to bear whatever comes, success or failure. Education is to recapture the striving for excellence found not only in the Greek but the Hebraic tradition. Instead of power in the sense of a strategic mastery over the destiny of other people and a position from which they can be pushed around, training is to emphasize the ability to function to the limits of one's power. The cult of money is to be replaced by work and love, security by risk. The "fun imperative" will give way to the adventure of ideas. Instead of constant quest for happiness, education will value the whole affectional range of life as well as the capacity to face tragedy and death. Instead of the cult of the individual as an atomistic unity, we will capture the sense of connection and ability to identify with others.

Max Lerner's proposal for re-evaluation places education in a moral if not a religious context. It raises a whole host of unanswered questions which concern Professor Ulich of Harvard in his *Philosophy of Education*. Ulich finds that the predominately pragmatic approach has not asked, "Why and toward what ends do we educate?" [12] Such questions have been answered in the past from the Hebrew-Christian heritage as well as Greek philosophy. Ulich believes that the fundamental challenge does not come from pragmatism, which lacks a firm intellectual position and any abiding intellectual goals. The deeper challenge is the autonomous attitude proposed by a philosopher like Nietzsche; the basic question is not usefulness but transcendence. Christopher Dawson argues convincingly that Western culture is an organic unity, nurtured fundamentally by faith commitments. [13] The experience of freedom which pragmatists such as Dewey value so highly has roots in the Hebrew-Christian as well as the Greco-Roman tradition. An institutionally more pluralistic religious situation does not vitiate this fact. Nor does it justify derogation of more traditional norms.

An especially valuable study of the role of religion in public education was made by a special committee of the American Council on Education. The committee, made up of Protestant, Roman Catholic and Jewish leaders, published its first report following the Second World War. Later studies considered the problem of professional and community attitudes. The committee report distinguished between "secularization"—that is, freedom from church control—and "secularism." The latter is a philosophy of life which has no place for religious creeds or for the institutions of worship. It denies the validity of religion in any of its historical forms and is in fact a rival faith. The committee commented, "We reject secularism as a philosophy of life and we cannot agree that it has ever been accepted as such by the American people." "If the churches and synagogues of America were fully convinced of the implications of the secularization of education, the popular mood would reflect that conviction in a stronger demand for its correction."

Much unnecessary controversy could be avoided if the committee's clarifications were accepted:

1. The problem is to find a way in public education to give due recognition to the place of religion in the culture and convictions of our people while at the same time safeguarding the separation of church and state.

2. The separation of American public education from church control was not intended to exclude all study of religion from the school program.

3. Teaching of a common core of religious beliefs in the public schools is not a satisfactory solution.

4. Teaching of "moral and spiritual" values cannot be regarded as an adequate substitute for an appropriate consideration of religion in the school program.

5. Teaching which opposes or denies religion is as much a violation of religious liberty as teaching which advocates or supports any particular religious belief.

6. Introducing factual study of religion will not commit the public schools to any particular religious belief.

7. The role of the school in the study of religion is distinct from, though complementary to, the role of the church.

8. The public school should stimulate the young toward a vigorous, personal reaction to the challenge of religion.

9. The public school should assist youth to have an intelligent understanding of the historical and contemporary role of religion in human affairs.[14]

The committee believes that the secularization of education has gone so far in the direction of secularism as to have far outrun the intentions of the founders of the public schools. It believes that it is important to understand that the separation of the public school from church control was not the result of a growing irreligiousness on the part of the American people. In fairness to the complexities of the problem, it must be noted that "the immediate cause of the exclusion of religious teaching from the schools was sectarian conflict."

A vital religious faith permeates every cultural good and influences every aspect of life. To those who take it seriously, religious faith is the spiritual foundation of society and indispensable to an enduring social structure.[15]

To be sure, the public schools cannot take up the full commitment of the religious community. Yet they hold so large a power over the concerns of youth that they cannot be indifferently neutral. Study must be objective and guided by educational interests. It needs to be made clear that secular control does not necessarily imply secularism or the dogmatic denial of religion.

The committee defends the position that concern for religion in public education is not a violation of the separation of church and state.

But it is essential that it be understood not as an absolute —which it tends to become in much current controversial literature—but as a broad principle of varying application, the essence of which is the preservation of the maximum religious freedom.

The first point to observe is that even separation in terms of control is a relative conception. There is no such thing as a completely free church in a free society . . . religion in America today plays a considerable role in governmental affairs.

We do not suggest that those who regard the introduction of religious subject matter into the schools as inherently destructive of freedom should abate their opposition in deference to a principle of local control. We do urge, first, the abandonment of an appeal to nonexistent precedent in support of an extreme secularist position; secondly, a frank facing of a problem that is all of a piece with the extension of democratic control of education and with the steady widening of the scope of the school program.

The core of meaning in the doctrine of separation of church and state we believe to be this: there shall be no ecclesiastical control of political functions; there shall be no political dictation in the ecclesiastical sphere except as public safety or public morals may require it. This doctrine may not be invoked to prevent public education from determining on its own merits the question how the religious phases of the culture shall be recognized in the school program.[16]

The committee of the American Council on Education is careful to point out that teaching about religion in public education is not by itself a full learning experience. Nonetheless, the minimum responsibility of education is for the breaking down of prejudice and ignorance. It is acknowledged that members of some denominations will not welcome the communication of knowledge about religion to their children through the public schools. Is the proposal to include it in the curriculum a halfway house or, more than this, an attempt to do the work of the churches or synagogues? The report argues that religion is not something to be added on to the curriculum. It is inseparably bound up with the culture as a whole. In social studies, history, literature and music as well as the problems of world culture, religious questions inevitably appear. Church and synagogue, like other institutions, are dependent on the school for the basic educational equipment of their people. To include religion is not to ask for special favor. "Youth should be made appreciatively aware of those aspects of individual and social living which, with abundant social sanction, they (religions) have sought to serve." The report advocates experiment in different local situations, as conditions vary from community to community.

The committee envisages teacher education as the central focus for implementing its proposals. A large number of teachers are already broadly interested and informed; others can be trained. The committee advocates consultation with leaders of all major religious groups as points of view are developed in university training as well as in curriculum construction. The pluralism of American life has been enriched by the presence of a variety of points of view. Judaism, Roman Catholicism and Protestantism have all contributed to the background of our culture. The primary purpose of any such consultation should be unqualifiedly educational and not an attempt to effect conversion to any single group. It also must be kept clear that cooperation between church and school does not imply identity or control of one by the other. The underlying unity of conviction of Protestants, Roman Catholics and Jews has become more evident than before in the face of secular threats such as totalitarianism. It should be strengthened, but it should not at any point be made intolerant of persons who support democracy on wholly secular grounds.

What we do contend insistently is that in the effort to build a democratic society a failure to capitalize the ideals of ethical monotheism, the teachings of Judaism and of Christianity, the tough fibre of that integrity which made the church resist, more effectively than any other institution, the Nazi tyranny in Europe—a failure to preserve such great assets is sheer cultural madness.

The exclusion of religion from the public schools which so largely prevails today results in its relegation in the minds of youth to a position of relative unimportance. This runs counter, we believe, to the intention of the American school system from the beginning.

The religious community itself, which must bear a large part of the blame for the extremes to which secularization has gone, has an important part to play in their correction. Everything we have suggested can be blocked or nullified by sectarian bitterness, suspicion and fear.

The intensive cultivation of religion is, and always has been, the function of religious institutions. To create an awareness of its importance is the responsibility of public education. In creating such an awareness the school is but rounding out its educational task, which culminates in the building of durable convictions about the meaning of life and personal commitments based on them.[17]

NOTES

1. James B. Conant, *Slums and Suburbs* (New York: McGraw-Hill, 1961).
2. Max Lerner, *Education and a Radical Humanism* (Columbus: Ohio State University Press, 1962), p. 28.
3. *Ibid.*, p. 29.
4. Lawrence A. Cremin, *The Transformation of the School: Progressivism in American Education, 1876–1957* (New York: Knopf, 1961), pp. 347–351.
5. Conant, *op. cit.*
6. Cremin, *op. cit.*
7. John Dewey, "The Teacher and His World," *Problems of Men* (New York: Philosophical Library, 1946), pp. 70ff.
8. Myron Lieberman, *The Future of Public Education* (Chicago: University of Chicago Press, 1960).
9. Lerner, *op. cit.*, pp. 30–31.
10. *Ibid.*, pp. 29–30.
11. *Ibid.*, p. 4.
12. Robert Ulich, *Philosophy of Education* (New York: American Book Co., 1961).
13. Christopher Dawson, *The Crisis of Western Education* (New York: Sheed and Ward, 1961), pp. 119f.
14. ACE Studies: Reports of Committees and Conferences, XI, No. 26 (Washington, D.C., April, 1947), pp. 49f.
15. *Ibid.*
16. *Ibid.*, pp. 23–25.
17. *Ibid.*, pp. 47, 49, 53, 54.

5

A Place for Religion in the Schools

Professor Philip H. Phenix, a member of the faculty of Teachers College, Columbia University, has written a discerning study entitled *Religious Concerns in Contemporary Education*.[1] His attitude reflects the increased openness toward religion in educational theory. Professor Phenix finds that the present period is characterized not only by a world-wide awakening of mankind to the importance of education, but by a renewal of interest in religion. He urges that the two cannot be separated absolutely, especially in view of the crisis in civilization through which mankind at present is passing.

Modern man is in search of a faith. He is eagerly, even desperately, seeking for honest and dependable answers to questions about the meaning of life. He perceives the need for reliable foundations upon which to effect a secure yet creative civilization.

Professor Phenix follows Paul Tillich in regard to ultimacy and shows its relation to education in terms of (1) inquiry, that is, breaking the bonds of the purely customary

55

and routine; (2) desire, in its infinite outreach; and (3)
decision.[2] He uses a variety of descriptive terms to show
what it means. Like Tillich, he regards it as having an
existential character. Ultimacy seeks the most important—
supreme worth or value. It probes beneath the surface in
a dimension of depth, but it also looks for totality or com-
prehensiveness. It has to do with origins as well as destiny.
Ultimacy is in search of relationships as well as of prospects
for the future. Professor Phenix concludes that the relation
between religion and education is an inevitable one:

> Religion as ultimate concern therefore provides the large
> framework within which education occurs. It determines per-
> spective and basic orientation. It governs emphasis and fixes
> trends. Religious concern (whether or not recognized and des-
> ignated as such) is the motive which actuates the educator and
> produces the general pattern of work.[3]

Phenix finds that whatever becomes ultimate for the human person is his religion; whatever he trusts is his faith.
Of course, all ultimacy is not necessarily Jewish or Christian. Islam, Hinduism and Buddhism all have dimensions
of ultimacy; modern secularism often ignores such meaning!
The American ideals of equality, justice and respect for
the individual, suggested by phrases such as "in God we
trust" and "this nation under God," have a faith derivation
and suggest religious dedication. The religious meanings
which the school must seek to transmit derive from the
larger community. What ought to be the relation between
religion and education? Professor Phenix finds that the
problem is not an easy one. Practically, one must consider
not only religion and education but churches and schools.
He rightly emphasizes that religion is intrinsic and not just
instrumental to the school experience; it is not simply to
be used but is a dimension of meaning in its own right.
The school has an originative, creative role as religious

values come alive and are apprehended positively. It has a right to autonomy in teaching about religion, but not without consideration of particular traditions. Phenix's position is a discerning one, as compared with other less sensitive interpretations. Too often, public education has supposed that questions of ultimate meaning and destiny can be solved by common sense, if not by democratic consensus. In fact, it has depended on a common faith more than on either science or democracy. This faith has not been nurtured by pragmatism, as Dewey supposed, but by the great religions!

With the rise and dominance of pragmatism, both instruction and content in the public school have undergone far-reaching changes. Religious dimensions of "ultimacy" were ignored. No doubt, a new educational orientation arose in response to new conditions. Sectarian religious content seemed irrelevant; more important was a positive, world-affirming religious attitude. The developing theory and practice together reflected the spirit and dynamics of the culture which they served. Older patterns of learning and morality were regarded as outmoded in a technological, urbanized society. The expanded contact with other countries in the period of the two world wars led to an increased diversity of norms within the country itself. Less absolutistic patterns of judgment were necessary in differing situations which required fresh and dynamic approaches. With the breakdown of long-established social structures, much of the traditional ethical instruction of earlier eras was abandoned.

Not only was education to present the facts of contemporary science and technology; the child was to learn to live with his fellows in community and life-adjustment. Pragmatists interpreted the schoolroom as a kind of model laboratory for democracy.[4] A child was to be given practice in solving problems for himself. Encouraged with a minimum of direction or moralizing, he would mature into responsible citizenship. Of course, the classroom would be free of religious conflicts. The wisdom of the past was regarded as less important than adaptation to present group demands and circumstances. Theodore Brameld, in his *Philosophies of Education in Cultural Perspective,* urges that pragmatism is an outlook which makes possible transition between two great cultural configurations: Western culture is shifting rapidly away from those ways of living achieved in the past, moving quickly to new ways of living that are still to be achieved in the future.[5] But how are these changed ways to be evaluated?

In fact, the alienation of education from religion can be regarded as normal only by pragmatism or an overt secularism. More normal is a positive relation between them; this remains true even in a pluralistic society. Education has not only the goal of learning facts but that of developing character. It is not simply that a fund of knowledge is to be attained, but powers of decision and judgment are to be strengthened in the training of the will. Integrity and responsibility most of all are its legitimate goals. The citizen, be he child or adult, is called upon to live in an increasingly complex society. Even when temptations of the grossest sort are glorified before him in mass media of communication, is the school never to protest in terms of religious norms of abiding right and wrong? Yet it must deal with character. Granted that the issues are not exclusively religious, but psychological and sociological! Consensus never reaches to the root of the moral life, much less to its creativity. When religion is ruled out, a whole dimension of meaning and experience of the life of the child is disregarded. Creativity and responsibility, issues of good and evil, life and death, may be excluded from teaching but not from living.

Professor Phenix has emphasized that the scope of reli-

gion in education is much broader than knowledge of the
Bible or even particular theological traditions of interpretation. It has to do as well with the context and principles
of education, including what is often called natural theology. Whenever the total patterns of thought and personal
decision are open to evaluation, religious implications inevitably appear. T. M. Greene has pointed out ably that the
roots of our civilization are Greco-Roman and Hebrew-
Christian as well as democratic and scientific.[6] The primary
weakness of pragmatism, in the larger view, is its almost
total neglect of the first two basic sources of our culture.
It refuses to see the last two in their historical context and
relationship to the first. A genuinely humanistic education
must consider the whole Western intellectual tradition, including art, literature and history. Dewey regarded scientific
experiment as the prototype of all knowledge. He interpreted a large part of Western intellectualism as "armchair
philosophy." In its place, he offered a call for action: we
learn to do by doing! What will be the result in curriculum
and outlook if education takes on a more humanistic character? Suppose it is agreed that its major aim should be to
make students aware of the achievements of the past as
much as to prepare them for the future? Literature, history
and art must assuredly have a major place in teaching.

Do not the humanities belong more to college instruction than to the public school experience? This question
needs to be faced clearly in present discussion of educational
policy. Paul Tillich distinguishes between education as initiation into a particular community, especially a religious
one, and humanistic training. One seeks to perpetuate a
given type of devotion. The other attempts to explore and
realize the fullest potentialities of the human being, potentialities which may be implicitly religious. The distinction
between the two is not necessarily absolute. Christopher
Dawson has stated that it was the tradition of humanism

which continued to unite European education in spite of the
Reformation and the wars of religion.[7] Such humanism
was not simply secular! We believe that in present circumstances, humanism and religion have a common cause
against secularism. Pupils are already aware of responsibility
and guilt, love and hate. These are presented daily, often in
perverse form, in television and motion pictures. The responsibility of education is to develop tastes, values, perspective and judgment in relation to these experiences. A
new humanism is called for to replace an outmoded pragmatism.

A perennial value of great literature is that it presents
the human scene, good and evil, hope and disappointment,
with a sense of perspective which is not just pragmatic.
Temptation, freedom and finitude are illumined rather
than covered up. The perennial themes of drama, poetry
and the novel make clear that we cannot master fully the
human condition—by knowledge, technology or statecraft.
Existence under contemporary conditions is easily externa-
lized and mechanized. The literary tradition demands that
one look within; understanding is not simply imposed from
without. Subtlety of meaning goes with artistic insight. Literary imagination cannot regard life as a problem to be
solved as in mathematics or technology. Rather, it understands it as what Marcel has called a "mystery" to be
lived with. Freedom by its very nature makes demands
on the human person. Moral insight comes from seeing
life with sensitivity as well as critical reflection. Artistic
insight can show the variety of risks and temptations,
the depths of human evil as well as the hope of beatitude.
In this way it raises what are in the end humanistic
and religious questions! It does not allow that the last
is necessarily the best in a naïve doctrine of progress.
Without ultimate concern for the worth of human life,

death, freedom, responsibility, the stature of literature itself is lost by its lack of insight.

History more than literature deals with "facts." It is a discipline which guards against the fancies of the imagination or literary symbols. Ought one to suppose that it has any intrinsic relation to religion? If the question of motivation or norms is raised, religious questions emerge. Is it fair to judge the meaning of history simply from our present place? The study of history helps one to know himself and his society. At the very least, one ought to ask that instruction treat particular histories in the context of world events. The larger cultural question remains as to why Western thought is so historically conscious as compared with Indian or Chinese interpretation. The answer in part is assuredly its Hebrew-Christian heritage which takes such a realistic view of time and change. It is an oversimplification to describe the Western view of time as linear and the Eastern view as cyclical. Yet the fact remains that Western religious ideas conditioned our culture to regard history as dynamic rather than static. Certainly, the motivation of historical change is not simply a religious one. But any possible explanation must use inclusive symbols and perspectives.

One should examine the forms of understanding through which we view the world. Secularism is always in danger of mistaking temporal success for the final good. A particular history is enlarged world-wide in a context of nationalism in secular education. High religion refuses to allow us to make our present position absolute as the center of meaning or the sole standard of right and wrong.[8] It knows that evil is persistent; put down in one form, it reappears in another. Not only does history not solve all its own problems, it creates new ones as well. Our judgments and perspectives must be put in relation to those of other epochs, and finally to transcendent ethical norms. Such perspective, not easy to attain, is nonetheless required by the Hebrew-Christian tradition and may yet lead to a more comprehensive view of man and his possibilities. Western thought has taken history seriously for religious and not just practical reasons. To accept the ambiguity of history, its evil and threat of meaninglessness, is easier if one recognizes an abiding Good beyond it.

Of course, such cultural achievements as painting, sculpture, music and drama carry humanistic meanings on virtually every side. To be sure, all that is done in these media is not explicitly religious. Our question is whether one can teach about them inclusively in a simply secular context. So much of art implies ultimate concern. At times, art and religion are separated from each other; the artist has a legitimate freedom of his own. At other times, art highlights areas of deep religious concern from which it receives inspiration. In its own way, it is often not only an expression of religious motivation, but a bridge to religious meaning. How will one explain the medieval cathedrals, the painting and sculpture of Michelangelo or the masses of a Mozart, Schubert or Beethoven? Simply by economic or social factors? Whatever else is present, there is a deep level of imagination and sensitivity which relates them to what Tillich terms, "ultimate concern."

Pragmatism often minimized the intrinsic meanings of literature and history in an appeal to natural science. The latter is regarded as a more objective mode of understanding and knowledge. But it, too, stands in a tradition without which it is inexplicable. Much of so-called objective science is really the history of science. Is scientific research simply disinterested and objective? Does it not demand personal integrity on the part of the investigator? More than this, are not sensitivity and imagination of high importance in its creative achievement? Apart from the question as to whether scientific method is simply empirical, one must ask whether it can solve all of the problems of personal existence. In fact, research now claims less exhaustive knowledge of the universe than in the last century, in view of the revolution in physics brought about by the relativity and quantum theory. It is much less certain than before that everything can be explained with complete objectivity apart from the observer. One must continue to ask about the meaning of life for the human person. Of course, teaching must continue to be scientific as well as humanistic, practical as well as theoretical. The educational concern is for the context in which these are to be set.

A balanced Christian humanism—implicitly a critique of pragmatism—was set forth in Jacques Maritain's important study, *Education at the Crossroads.*[9] Education, Maritain believes, must appeal to spontaneous impulses and imagination as well as to the desire for knowledge. There is need for vision, not just collecting of facts or opinions. At the same time, education seeks to foster internal unity in man. "What matters most in the life of reason is intellectual insight or intuition. There is no training or learning of that." [10] Subject matter taught should equip the child with ordered knowledge, so that he may advance toward wisdom in age. Learning begins with experience, but it must complete itself in reason. It seeks to develop acceptance of one's own existence as well as of other persons. More than we realize, we are dependent on the wisdom of the past. The pupil, allegedly understood from experimental science alone, is measured and directed efficiently, but toward what goal? Maritain's criticism of pragmatism is directed against its emphasis on the supremacy of means over ends. He argues that "the educational task is both greater and more mysterious and, in a sense, humbler than many imagine."

The self, freedom and value do not yield to simply quantitative measurement. To be sure, science provides ever increasing information, but it does not solve the problem of the nature and destiny of man.

A person possesses absolute dignity because he is in direct relationship with the realm of being, truth, goodness, and beauty, and with God, and it is only with these that he can arrive at his complete fulfillment. His spiritual fatherland consists of the entire order of things which have absolute value, and which reflect, in some manner, a divine Absolute superior to the world and which have a power of attraction toward this Absolute.[11]

Maritain protests against the notion that everything can be taught and learned. Judgment and will no more than real understanding, he argues, can be so communicated. Maritain describes education as an art, based on both nature and culture. It must give more attention to the dynamic factors of mind; truth comes from within and not just from without.

A large community of agreement remains in the Western world. There is a religious reason for the demand that education respect the deepest life and freedom of the child. He has a mysterious identity which cannot be controlled by technique alone. The child is plastic and susceptible to suggestion. As the teacher helps him to distinguish the true from the false, his personality is liberated. The teacher's goals have to do with love of truth, goodness and justice—inwardness and internalization of influence. Both teacher and learner are dynamic. In a sense, the teacher's role is really only secondary. The world of the child is one of imagination, rich vitality and intuitiveness. Judgment and intellectual strength have greater possibility for development in adolescence. Instead of burdening the intelligence, teaching should seek its liberation. Its goal is not only the development of strength, skill and accuracy of mental power, but possession of knowledge.

Maritain understands that there are different traditions

of educational practice in response to varied problems and needs. Teaching, he believes, must seek "to shape a particular child belonging to a given nation, a given social environment, a given historical age." [12] It must also seek to evoke universal and articulate appreciation of human achievements. It has responsibility for conveying the cultural heritage in living form. Teaching attempts to tap the dynamism of the developing character of the child, enriching it from the common experience of the past. It deals not only with traditions of earlier generations but with universal principles. To be sure, Maritain's comments reflect his European background, specifically his French training. But his criticism of pragmatism is not an attempt to impose a European pattern on the American situation.

Teaching achieves authentic motivation when it awakens a free love of truth on the part of the student. It must not only adapt itself to the natural interests of the pupil; when successful, it renews his purposes as well as establishes new ones. A complete and integral idea of man must come from philosophy, and ultimately from religion. It is not enough that the pupil adjust to existing conditions. Character achieves many-sidedness and richness as it develops norms which transcend present circumstances. Contrary to pragmatic doctrine, Maritain insists that ethics is not the product of social conditioning. It provides us with standards of judgment which are more than mores of the time. Education encourages moral growth as it trains the intelligence in love of truth. Faith in one's own primary capacities for truth is a presupposition of knowledge. When the full range of the intellect is denied, as in pragmatic reductionism, character itself is circumscribed, the natural outreach and creativity of the mind are limited. Yet respect for the uniqueness and dignity of each human person as well as the concern to develop a responsible citizen both imply moral norms.

Education must appeal to intelligence and will, seeking to develop strength of judgment as well as moral virtue. Maritain distinguishes carefully between two kinds of freedom. The free will which is a gift of nature to each man need not be won but is possessed already. By contrast, inner spiritual freedom, spontaneity and autonomy, is won through constant struggle. Pragmatism, emphasizing action, has neglected this second type of freedom, even as it has failed to identify even the first carefully. It limits truth to the useful, in effect denying the ideals of pure knowledge and moral perfection. Too often, the object to be taught is forgotten in concern for technique, in a cult of means. What is the goal of education—the result to be achieved? Contrary to pragmatic theory, it is true knowledge and insight. Truth is an infinite realm whose wholeness transcends all our powers of perception. Pragmatism, failing to grasp its dynamic unity, joins concern for useful techniques of mental training to scholarly skepticism!

NOTES

1. New York: Teachers College, Columbia University, 1959.
2. Paul Tillich, *Systematic Theology* (Chicago: University of Chicago Press, 1951), I, p. 12.
3. Phenix, *op. cit.*, p. 19.
4. John Dewey, *Experience and Education* (New York: Macmillan, 1938).
5. Theodore Brameld, *Philosophies of Education in Cultural Perspective* (New York: Holt, Rinehart and Winston, 1955), p. 91
6. Theodore Meyer Greene, *Our Cultural Heritage* (Houston: Elsevier Press, 1956).
7. Christopher Dawson, *op. cit.*, p. 36.
8. Herbert Butterfield, *Christianity and History* (London: Bell, 1950).
9. Jacques Maritain, *Education at the Crossroads* (New Haven: Yale University Press, 1943).
10. *Ibid.*, p. 43.
11. *Ibid.*, *p.* 8.
12. *Ibid.*, p. 1.

6

Comparative Education:
The Post-War German Experience

Comparative education, the study of methods of teaching and learning in different countries, has received new attention in the post-war period. Scholars have recognized the importance of particular national outlooks: School organization as well as the spirit and goals of teaching reflects the underlying beliefs of a government and its people. Increased attention is being given to the social and ideological bases of different educational systems. For example, totalitarian regimes have developed their traditions in conscious rejection of Western European humanism.

In comparative education, it is important to distinguish carefully between the practical and theoretical as well as between educational method and world view. Perennial problems of organization and method appear irrespective of the political or social context. For example, what are the prerequisites for effective teaching in terms of adequate facilities as well as the planned, graded structure of curriculum? Yet questions of method cannot be separated completely from ideas and loyalties which are valued in the

classroom. The educator is more than a technician. He is
not dealing simply with things, but seeks to develop a relationship of trust, rapport and mutual effort in the school
community.

Rather than surveying Western European school policy
in general, this chapter will consider the changes brought
by a now defunct totalitarianism, Nazism, in the German
educational outlook. Germany even more than England has
been a creative source of ideas and traditions for public
education in the United States. Prussia developed an effective system of general state-supported education, with religious freedom, in advance of both France and England.
Horace Mann visited Germany before he organized the
public schools of Massachusetts. Although he criticized the
lack of political freedom under the monarchy, he nevertheless appropriated much from his European experience.
American university organization owes a great deal to German methods of scholarship. Specialized faculties of higher
learning have often been modelled on German research
institutes. It is of historical interest that a considerable number of American educators were sent to the defeated country
at the beginning of the Occupation. Their attempt to remake the values and ideals of the German schools was ineffective.[1] In the end, it was the Germans themselves who
reconstituted their school system, drawing on their own
traditions. The over-all school reform for which many non-
German observers had hoped, did not come about. Part of
the explanation is to be found in the fact that the West
German Federal Republic does not centralize political control as much as France. Moreover, the outlook of the
occupying powers varied in their respective zones. Of
course, the Germans maintained their own educational traditions in the West more than in the East. A common school
has been organized under Soviet influence. The question

of whether it has brought about needed restructuring has become secondary to issues of academic freedom!

Why did a nation as cultured as Germany surrender its educational system to the Nazis? Foreign observers all too easily overlook the virtually irresistible power of the police state as it crushed all protest, educational or religious. In general, American concern for Western democratic conviction has been effective in post-war education, but not in acceptance of scientism or pragmatism. The larger humanistic tradition is still valued highly. Only specially able students expect to enter the university, and it is recognized that there is no substitute for earnest study. The school remains a basic social agency in spite of the charges and counter charges which followed a bitter war experience. Contemporary German pedagogy does not regard education primarily as an agency of reform. It is critical of any utopianism which regards education as a means for ending all problems and settling every issue.

In general, schools are divided confessionally at the primary level: Roman Catholic, Protestant and secular. However, there are also some Christian community schools attended by pupils of both confessions. Maximum pressure for the exclusion of religion came under the Weimar Republic. The position of church leadership was stronger following the Second World War, as it became the one remaining voice which could speak effectively to the occupying powers for the people. The German mood from the Nazi experience has been one of realism. School instruction is understood as an institutional means of conveying the cultural heritage as well as of developing necessary skills, both general and professional. A recent survey of educational theory emphasizes that teaching cannot expect to change human nature; in essence, the person remains the same.[2] Moreover, his freedom for development through

education is limited. It is an abuse of state power to suppose that public education can mold the pupil in any way
it wishes. The state does not have the right to determine
his morals or religion apart from the home and church.
Together with them, it must seek to exemplify the respect
for truth and freedom upon which democracy rests.

There has been a drastic criticism of earlier educational
practice from a renewed democratic and religious consciousness. For example, Theodor Litt has pointed out tellingly
the discrepancy between educational ideals and historical
conditions in the early part of the century.[3] He argues
convincingly for a more relevant and socially responsible
view but not for "democratic utilitarianism." Modern German educational theory is especially indebted to the philosophy of Wilhelm Dilthey, who insisted on a dynamic but
not relativistic view of historical development.[4] For example,
he pointed out that educational ideals have different cultural
forms and goals in various epochs. The classical legacy of
Greek and Roman antiquity was modified radically in medieval Christendom and again in the Reformation. Modern
forces such as the rise of the middle class as well as technology have brought changed goals. Education is to enrich
the limited perspectives of a particular era by appreciation
for the diversity of historical experience, not to reduce their
range in parochialism—much less to exploit them for usefulness. Western European thought remains deeply indebted
to the Greek ideal of *Paedeia* which self-consciously made
education more than technique or utility. Intellectual and
moral traits of the good man are developed together through
disciplined training. To be sure, the Greek context of the
ideal was one of self-realization rather than of grace. Yet
the ideal was appropriated by Protestant education under
Melanchthon as well as by the Jesuits in the post-Reformation
period.

Characteristically, German scholars have given special attention to the methods and scope of comparative education. Professor Friedrich Schneider describes what he calls the "educational drive." [5] The power of a particular school system, he argues, arises from a complex of factors, geographical, economic, governmental and religious. Educational effectiveness varies from era to era as well as from society to society. The problem is made more complex by the fact that an open pluralistic society conveys its traditions in a different way than a more static one—for example, Chinese Confucian society. Moreover Western democratic practice is complicated by the presence of a plurality of educational agencies—radio, television, motion pictures—which are beyond the direct control of school authorities. By contrast, modern totalitarianism has concentrated its teaching program in a single unified pattern of direction and allows less variety. In fact, particular educational polity reflects not only social and political conditions, but the maturity of a people as well. Although modern pedagogy generally has been structured according to a particular national heritage, it cannot avoid the larger historical issues; for example, its relation to the heritage of Christendom. Overshadowing all differences between aristocratic and more equalitarian ideals is the rejection of the Western intellectual tradition in modern totalitarianism. Of course, one must be careful not to oversimplify issues by limiting comparative education to either political or religious themes.

Patterns of classification vary from one interpreter to another. It is often pointed out that there are at least four different outlooks which continue to compete against each other. The theistic, primarily Christian view, characterized by a strong personalism, is more clearly recognized than before. Its legacy remains even for those who no longer accept its faith premises. Often, it has been joined with a humanistic ideal which envisages the self-development of both the individual and society. The humanistic, rational ideal encourages a many-sided, harmonious person. Its sense of conscious formation and discipline stands in contrast with the naturalistic outlook of such a thinker as Rousseau. His essentially romantic ideal was that the child must be freed from the corrupting effects of culture for the development of his own intrinsically good powers. This ideal has been strongly influential in American pragmatism. By contrast, traditional humanism has a particular moral teleology, determined by ethical ideals. Recent interpretation emphasizes that it does not necessarily regard human nature as a predetermined whole. Humanism seeks to develop personal structures which will so organize it as to liberate its creativity. Duty and discipline are not centered simply on interest, but determined more primarily by intellectual judgment. All three positions, which have found expression in Western democratic thought, in principle reject the totalitarian claim that human nature can be reshaped to conform to the wishes of the absolute state.[6]

Rousseau in his "Savoyard Vicar's Profession" expressed the faith in man's own ability to determine the center of meaning and value which has been reflected in secular education. The Vicar's confession is made by a priest to a young boy, just at daybreak in a beautiful river valley. The clergyman reports that he still continues to administer rites and ceremonies, to affirm orally the dogmas of the Church. His real belief, however, is in a universal reality and goodness which extends beyond particular creeds, cutting around their historical claims. It roots itself in a faith still deeper than any of these: the humanity of man. Older cultural restraints and claims for redemption are irrelevant in view of the innate goodness of man. The traditions and authority of the past have held man in chains. Education is to liberate him from these bonds. Later, the philosophy of self-sufficient, autonomous man was made into a philosophy of history by the French positivist Auguste Comte: Human thought was once governed by myth and theology; a second stage transposed religious insight into philosophical thought forms and language. Finally, in the modern period, science replaced philosophy. In the place of traditional faith in God, Comte proposed a new religion of humanity. Of course, such a religion has not long sustained itself in the face of modern skepticism, much less totalitarianism.

Shocked by the renewal of German paganism under the Nazis, a new Christian realism recognizes the "demonic" possibilities of life without the ethical restraints of the high religions. Professor Romano Guardini tells about living in a small community in Bavaria at the end of the Second World War, after he had been deposed from his teaching post in Berlin by the Nazis.[7] In spite of the difficulties of transportation, a school teacher travelled by motorcycle from Ulm to visit him. The teacher's question was the following: "What can we expect from German education in the future?" Guardini's answer was simply: truth. Both men had experienced the warping effect of ideology and propaganda as they minimize judgment and intellectual insight. Both also knew that untruth cannot be overcome simply by an appeal to the useful. The essentially religious bases of truth become clear in the face of threats to the integrity of teaching and learning. All meaning does not lie simply under human control.

Much of nineteenth-century theory of knowledge attempted to use scientific method as its guide. Now interest has significantly shifted away from this more impersonal model to problems of historical existence. Existentialism has set the problems of teaching in a new context. This type of philosophy is concerned with the orientation which Paul Tillich defined in terms of "ontological" as distinguished from "technological reason." [8] Technological reason, in Tillich's definition, is exercised in thinking which organizes and uses data in the world, unconcerned with ultimate truth.

Its remarkable genius is evident in the success of modern science. Ontological reason seeks to understand reality; its interest is not just the useful. Instead, it explores the basic perspectives of knowledge in the belief that it can find intrinsic meaning. The non-Christian German philosopher Martin Heidegger has emphasized how much has been lost by turning to technology alone for the solution of all human problems.[9] Psychological and sociological analysis, by themselves, he argues, provide no escape from nihilism. However, Heidegger's effect on pedagogy has been a very limited one. Bollnow argues that this is the case because he has not given a sufficiently positive doctrine of truth.[10]

It is clear that two world wars have destroyed the faith in progress on which so much of secular humanistic as well as naturalistic educational theory was premised. The idea of progress carries significant meaning, even though it has been often abused. As a symbol, it seems to signify that history is like an army marching forward. The linear view of the Hebrew-Christian tradition is accepted, but without religious eschatology. Morally, progress is invoked to imply that evil is diminishing, if not inevitably, at least by human effort. The idea is applied not only to the expansion of knowledge, but to cultural and moral development. A more critical judgment may lead to the view that moral progress is ambiguous; there is growth of both good and evil in history. Nor ought Christian world-affirmation to be confused with this secular claim. It is not based on any temporal development alone, but faith that the world is good because God is both its creator and redeemer.

It is necessary to distinguish at least four different levels of interpretation, in order to evaluate what is valid and what is not, in judgments of progress.[11] In areas of technology and science, knowledge is cumulative and can be represented virtually as a straight line upward through history. At a second level, the organization of society, it is not difficult to identify increased efficiency of political structures. Empires have greater effectiveness of administration than before. Their power to evoke loyalty or creativity among their subjects cannot be judged as easily, however. Surely, it is not to be identified simply with the expansion of power. With respect to personal moral growth, a third level, there continue to be tyrants and criminals. Critical appraisal requires a more complex hierarchy of values than is suggested by the idea of progress. Finally, at the religious level, it is of very limited relevance. The history of religion yields no simple developmental interpretation. Naturally, one distinguishes monotheism from primitivism, the ethical from the base. However, Western theism is not premised on human development alone, but on divine disclosure. Too often the idea of progress, like science and democracy, is misused to cover up the necessity of moral decisions as well as complex historical and philosophical evaluations.

Contemporary European philosophy of education seeks to avoid one-sidedness in theory of knowledge as well as in historical interpretation. The inductive empirical approach is applied with more self-criticism and rigor than by the pragmatists. More deductive, rationalistic analysis is not regarded as being as exhaustive as has often been supposed. Both are to be supplemented by the intuitive, so-called phenomenological method, which ranges over the widest possible expression of the human spirit in art and literature as well as philosophy and religion. A balanced, creative interpretation of present German philosophical interest appears in the study of Professor Gadamer of the University of Heidelberg entitled *Method and Truth*.[12] Professor Gadamer emphasizes that knowledge is in a tradition; our understanding is not in fact timeless, but historical. Structural moments give expression to abiding meanings. Education should compel the student to self-examination, responsibility and moral judgment. He has become self-critical

when he questions the limits of knowledge as well as the
meaning of existence. We ought not to expect that the
answer will be just a rationalistic generalization any more
than a judgment of usefulness. Teacher and pupil are to be
encouraged in dialogue, not just about the useful but about
intrinsic meanings. Prerequisite is a desire for encounter
with reality in its personal dimensions and not simply an
ideological world view. In terms of personal life, history is
not just an idea or a problem to be solved but a reality to be
lived with.

The relevance of a value-oriented "existential" approach
can be illustrated specifically from post-war attempts at political education. The earlier training in citizenship, patriotism and love for the fatherland, under the monarchy, is now
regarded in Germany as inadequate. New democratic forms
of life demand mature evaluation of issues as well as a
personal sense of political responsibility. Is it possible to
teach critically about current events as well as the national
heritage? How can the school encourage a spirit of tolerance
and reality without utopian idealism? Can it avoid indoctrination of a new democratic ideology which may be as irrelevant to present needs as past programs? For younger students,
heroes are important as models. For olders ones, knowledge
of history and geography can help in the development of
perspective. Yet more than method is at stake, namely, the
truth. Democracy cannot live merely on the useful, any more
than on irrelevant idealism. The importance of moral sanctions as well as the insights of the philosophical and religious
traditions becomes clear in the face of totalitarian threats.

NOTES

1. Robert Ulich, *The Education of Nations* (Cambridge: Harvard University Press, 1961), p. 212.
2. Wolfgang Scheibe, *Die Pädagogik im XX Jahrhundert* (Stuttgart: Klett,
1960), p. 110.

3. Theodor Litt, *Freiheit und Lebensordnung, Zur Philosophie und Päda-gogik der Demokratie* (Heidelberg: Quelle & Meyer, 1962).

4. Andreas Flitner, *Wege zur Pädagogischen Anthropologie* (Heidelberg: Quelle & Meyer, 1963). Article by Friedrich Kümmel, "Kulturanthro-pologie," pp. 163–187.

5. Friedrich Schneider, *Vergleichende Erziehungswissenschaft, Geschichte, Forschung, Lehre* (Heidelberg: Quelle & Meyer, 1961).

6. Theodor Wilhelm, *Pädagogik der Gegenwart* (Stuttgart: Kröner, 1963).

7. Romano Guardini, *Sorge um den Menschen* (Wurzburg; Werkbund, 1962), p. 140.

8. Paul Tillich, *Systematic Theology* (Chicago: University of Chicago Press, 1951), I, pp. 72–73.

9. Martin Heidegger, *Die Technik und die Kehre* (Pfullingen: Neske, 1962).

10. Otto Friedrich Bollnow, *Existenzphilosophie und Pädagogik* (Stuttgart: Kohlhammer, 1959), pp. 107, 117.

11. Reinhold Niebuhr, *Faith and History* (New York: Scribner, 1949).

12. Hans-Georg Gadamer, *Warheit und Methode, Grundzüge einer philos-ophischen Hermeneutik* (Tübingen: Mohr, 1960).

7

The Case for Christian Humanism

One of the most important books written by the German philosopher Romano Guardini is entitled *The End of the Modern World*.[1] The title reflects the widespread realization in Western European thought that a renewal of humanism on secular bases is no longer possible. The issues which confront our society are fundamentally religious; the choice is between respect for the holy and life in a tradition with its values and norms—or nihilism! T. S. Eliot has argued that a culture with a Christian background, now posing as neutral, cannot do so indefinitely.[2] To suppose that we can have a society of integrity with a creative intellectualism, apart from living religious symbols, seems to him historically mistaken. Unless education is guided by a Christian philosophy of life, he believes, it becomes "merely a term comprehending a variety of unrelated subjects undertaken for special purposes or none at all." Christopher Dawson has pointed out the danger for culture in the joining of dogmatic religion with a secular utilitarian ethos.[3] In the end, responsible intellectualism is not required. Religion is no longer a force capable of transforming society. The only viable alternative to such a situation is for Christians to understand the history of their own tradition.

Reinhold Niebuhr has described the Hebrew-Christian view of human nature and destiny as delimited from modern secular interpretation in two directions: against a naturalism which denies all transcendence and against a rationalism which, regarding man primarily as mind, expects to encompass all the mysteries of existence.[4] The Christian view of man denies neither nature nor reason. However, it sets their interpretation in a larger, more inclusive context than either extreme. It takes issue with a self-sufficient philosophy which regards man as his own beginning and end. Too often, such an interpretation oversimplifies questions of fate and destiny. The fact is that man has greater potentialities for evil than can be explained simply from nature as well as creative possibilities for fulfillment which cannot be achieved by reason alone.

The basic question is whether all possibilities and meanings are self-contained in man himself. Such a view is ultimately confining: man is bound to his own rules and resources. A more cosmic outlook affirms that good and evil are rooted in the universe. They are discovered rather than invented by man. Truth and falsehood, right and wrong, abide whatever we may do. Goodness remains even when apparently defeated in history. Such a view is really the more open one; man is not bound merely to himself. It belongs to theism's deepest insight that it understands that human dignity does not come just from man himself, but from God. Believing that man has an eternal destiny with God, Jews and Christians cannot think or act simply from expediency. The attempt to reduce man to a this-worldly creature whose morality is premised on common consent is the expression of a mistaken faith, not of scientific investigation.

Public opinion polls have reported, from time to time,

that a leading reason for dissatisfaction with the public schools arises from their lack of religious teaching.[5] The skepticism and indifference characteristic of many aspects of American life in the 1920's have been dissipated in the era of World War II. In an attempt to express the widespread concern for religion in education, various statements have been issued calling for the teaching of moral and spiritual values. One such statement was the background of the Regents' Prayer case before the Supreme Court. Supplementing an earlier pronouncement of November 30, 1951, the New York State Board of Regents issued the following recommendation on March 28, 1955:

That periods be set aside at frequent intervals during the school year which will be devoted to the intensive study of the foregoing and great American documents and pronouncements. The same will give to the student an understanding and appreciation of his role as an individual endowed by his Creator with inalienable rights and as a member of a group similarly endowed; of respect for others, particularly parents and teachers; of devotion to freedom and reverence for Almighty God. Thus, as we heretofore stated, "the school will fulfill its high function of supplementing the training of the home, ever intensifying in the child that love for God, parents and for home which is the mark of true character training and the sure guarantee of a country's welfare." [6]

The statement was very restricted with respect to curriculum; it explicitly advocated "teaching for" religion, although naturally in a very limited way. Especially in New York City, attempts to implement it were hindered by controversy between religious groups. Following the Supreme Court decision against the Regents' Prayer, professional educators have been distinguishing more carefully between "teaching for" and "teaching about" religion.[7]

The New York City experience should not be allowed to

discourage teachers and staffs in other communities. Religion in the public schools is in part a local problem; the Supreme Court has attempted to mark limits—not to exclude it entirely! Attitudes vary from community to community. The question is not whether there will be differences of opinion or even strong disagreement. It is rather in what context and in respect to what principles the struggle between different outlooks shall take place. Justice Jackson in his dissenting opinion in the Everson case wrote: "Our public school . . . is organized on the premise that secular education can be isolated from all religious teaching so that the school can inculcate all needed temporal knowledge and also maintain a strict and lofty neutrality to religion." [8] In the McCollum decision, however, he subsequently conceded that there are many reasons why it is not possible "completely to isolate and cast out of secular education all that some people may reasonably regard as religious instruction." He added: "One can hardly respect a system of education that would leave the student wholly ignorant of the currents of religious thought that move the world society, for a part in which he is being prepared." [9]

Christopher Dawson has made an important contribution to "teaching about" religion in the program he has proposed for including "Christian culture" in the curriculum. In the use of this term, he takes his cue in part from Toynbee: he does not limit it to literature or art forms, but gives major emphasis to social institutions and moral values. Only as we include Christianity in the subject matter of education, he argues, do we have a perspective for understanding the unity of our civilization:

One of the chief defects of modern education has been its failure to find an adequate method for the study of our own civilization. . . . Now the old humanist education, with all its limitations and faults, possessed something that modern education has lost. It possessed an intelligible form. . . . The organic unity of Western culture is so strong that even the modern developments of extreme nationalism have been incapable of creating any real cultural and spiritual autarky.[10]

Too often, the history of the modern era has been oversimplified, as it has been identified with a growing secularism. No more than the Marxist can the Western democratic educator avoid questions of the meaning of history; he must take care to avoid dogmatism. For example, one hears too often of a progressive development from medieval supernaturalism to Renaissance humanism, Enlightenment rationalism, and finally empirical science and modern technology. The Middle Ages is regarded as a kind of cultural vacuum between Rome and the Renaissance. Dawson writes:

This view, which necessarily ignores the achievements and even the existence of Christian culture, was passed on almost unchanged from the Renaissance to the eighteenth-century Enlightenment and from the latter to the modern secularist ideologies. And although today every instructed person recognizes that it is based on a completely erroneous view of history and very largely on a sheer ignorance of history, it still continues to exert an immense influence, both consciously and unconsciously, on modern education and on our attitude to the past.[11]

Moreover, if we desire to promote religious and intellectual understanding among the different religious groups within American society, surely the best way to do this is to understand and appreciate our own culture in all its depth and breadth. Without this full cultural awareness it is impossible either to interpret one's culture to others or to understand the problems of intercultural relations, problems which are of such incalculable importance for the future of the modern world.

I do not deny that there are great practical obstacles in the way of this study. The secularist is naturally afraid that it might be used as an instrument of religious propaganda, and he is consequently anxious to minimize the importance of the Christian element in our culture and exaggerate the gulf between modern civilization and the Christian culture of the past.

The Christian, on the other hand, is often afraid lest the historical study of Christian culture should lead to an identification of Christianity with a culture and a social system which belong to the dead past.[12]

Recognition that Christianity has its own authentic intellectualism is the presupposition of such study. It is not blind faith, much less primitivism or Biblicism. Christian theology developed its perspectives in dialogue with Greek philosophy as well as Judaism. It must be emphasized that the ideas of Socrates and Plato are not secular in the modern sense. Socrates drank the cup of hemlock in deep confidence in an abiding Good which would justify his cause. Plato's vision of a rational order, appropriated by later Christian interpretation, was not limited to nature; instead, it envisaged a transcendent meaning and reality. A good Providence not only structures being, but is actively at work in the world.[13] Of course, Greek perspectives concerning reason, morality and history differed from those of Hebraism. For example, there was not the strong voluntarism which characterizes Biblical religion. Socrates and Plato protested against polytheism, but did not achieve the full sense of transcendence of later Christian monotheism. Aristotle, although differing in outlook, was similarly motivated by a compelling concern for truth against all relativism. And thus Christians regarded Greek philosophy as a preparation for revelation.

Christianity began to make a new synthesis of culture even before the end of persecution. This fact can be seen most dramatically in the writings of Clement of Alexandria. The cathedral school which Clement directed had in part an apologetic purpose. Alexandria, with its world-renowned library, was a center of Greek humanism. Christians studying at the university needed help in understanding the larger cultural traditions in which they shared through education. Clement himself knew well the traditions of classical learning. Among his writings are a collection of suggestions which he did not defend, but put forth only as possibilities.[14] He began from the simple theistic premise that God is the author of all truth; all wisdom and knowledge come ultimately from the deity. Consequently, any worthwhile and valuable ideas, whatever context they may have, derive finally from this source.

Clement appropriated an Old Testament story and phrase: the Christians are to "spoil the Egyptians." As the Children of Israel left the land of bondage following the death of the Egyptian first-born, the masters gave their former slaves gifts from their own personal possessions. The Egyptians wished to hasten their former bondsmen out of the land, lest further plagues should come. So, too, Clement concluded that Christians are to appropriate whatever is of truth in Greek philosophy and culture for the glory of their faith. In retrospect, such a strategy seems virtually inevitable. Christian theology struggled to preserve its unique sense of personality and history against Gnostic eclecticism, yet it did not avoid synthesis with non-Jewish traditions. Following Clement, the Church Fathers of the period held increasingly that philosophy and religion stand in necessary relation. The theological premise for this view is that nature and grace are not antithetical; the first is fulfilled in the second.

Constantine's conversion and the end of persecution of Christians did not—as has so often been suggested—bring about the fall of Christianity. Rather, it required the new religion to face difficult problems: it could not remain simply personal or individualistic! Had it a social ethic? The moral directions for the new order of society were taken from both Greek philosophy, primarily Stoicism, and the Old Testament. Christians who had known persecution as individuals were now called on to lead the intellectual life of the Empire. Constantine hoped to find fresh strength for the rejuvenation of civilization by compelling the abandonment of polytheism and establishing state allegiance to the one true God. In the end, Rome fell to the barbarians, but the Christian Church continued even as Judaism had survived following the captivity. Christianity remained a vital force, even as expressed in feudal society. It struggled against the barbarian as it adapted itself to new social forms.

The *Cambridge Medieval History* comments on the relation of church and state as follows:

The effects of the Church upon the Empire may be summed up in one word, "freedom." In a word, authority was seen to be a form of service according to God's will and such service was freedom. It was, however, not from Seneca but from Christ and St. Paul that the Fathers took their constant theme of the essential equality of men before which slavery could not stand. . . . Not only did the Fathers establish the primitive unity and dignity of man, but seeing slavery as the result of the Fall, they found in the sacrifice of Christ a road to freedom that was closed to Stoicism.[16]

Christian intellectualism had its fullness in the Patristic period, in Augustine's synthesis of Hebraism and Hellenism. His *City of God* was written in answer to the question: Why does the Roman Empire continue to decline even after Christianity has been accepted? Augustine posited a continuing dualism between the city of man and the city of God, but his view was not essentially world-denying. He envisaged the growth of evil as well as of good in history. As Dawson points out, Augustine did not offer an empirical analysis as much as a vision of a larger whole with inclusive meanings. The city of God would triumph, but not without struggle. The Christian lives in both world and Church, but whereas the former is temporal and passing, the latter shares in the eternal. His religion brings a new understanding of freedom and reason in a radical personalism which relativizes earthly life. Man's life in history is meaningful because of the Providence of God. In contrast to the more naïve doctrines of inevitable progress, Christianity does not base its hope on history alone, but in an abiding good which transcends it. Augustine's interpretation of history has been rediscovered in criticism of the superficial view of evil in many modern secular theories.

Christianity insisted on the eternal destiny of each individual person, master or slave, male or female; it thus gave religious support to the dignity and worth of all men, regarding them as equals in the sight of God. According to much of Greek philosophy, by contrast, the wise man was to be valued and his rights respected, but not the slave or barbarian. Cochrane in his *Christianity and Classical Culture* has shown that the new faith brought a fresh ethos to culture and society—a revolutionary type of humanism.[17] History was no longer understood as essentially cyclical, but as a dynamic process with a beginning and end in the providence of God. The present was seen in relation to eternity, not self-complete but as a realm for responsible action. Freedom and nature were interpreted from destiny and grace. Civilized life was not negated but affirmed in a new context. The Christian view of existence found expression in art and philosophy as well as a new quest for political order.

Protestants have too often impoverished their own outlook by supposing that they could renounce earlier Christian history and avoid its problems. In fact, Augustine is the "Father" of both Roman Catholics and Protestants; together, they have drawn on his ideas. The high Middle Ages represented what Paul Tillich—not a Roman Catholic—has called a "theonomous" civilization.[18] There was unity of religious conviction as compared with later schism and secularism. Tillich describes the modern period as an era of "autonomous" culture; ultimate loyalty is not unified in a single transcendent Good. Moreover, he argues that it is not possible to sustain a creatively integrated civilization without the renewal of life at the religious level. The natural law doctrine, appropriated by later democratic theory, has its roots in earlier Christian interpretation. Otto von Gierke wrote in his *Political Theories of the Middle Ages:*

> In this Medieval Doctrine was already filled with the thought of the inborn and indestructible rights of the individual. . . . Moreover, a fugitive glance at Medieval Doctrine suffices to perceive how throughout it all, in sharp contrast to the theories of Antiquity, runs the thought of the absolute and imperishable value of the Individual; a thought revealed by Christianity. . . . That every individual by virtue of his eternal destiny is at the core somewhat holy and indestructible even in relation to the Highest Power; that the smallest part had a value of its own, and not merely because it is a part of a whole; that every man is to be regarded by the Community, never as a mere instrument, but also as an end; all this is not merely suggested, but is more or less clearly expressed.[19]

The Church not only preserved learning, but nurtured it in new centers, notably the rising universities. The medieval synthesis with the Greek and Roman classical heritage had its fullness in the writings of Aquinas. Natural and revealed truth, philosophy and theology were joined in a new and creative interpretation based, more than before, on the ideas of Aristotle. Maritain praises this cultural synthesis as representative of true Christian humanism, joining reason and faith, nature and grace, before their separation in the Renaissance and Reformation.[20] He does not suppose that its intellectualism can be applied without modification in the modern world. The cultural achievement of the high Middle Ages belonged to a particular era, not to be reconstituted again in full. Most important is that religion and culture

were understood as belonging together and not as mutually
hostile as is too often supposed by contemporary sectarianism, both secular and religious!

To suppose that the decline of medieval Christendom was
due simply to the Reformation is an oversimplification. Not
to be denied is the fact of change in government and social
life as well as science. New factors—economic, national and
geographic—for example, the discovery of the Americas, made
for different patterns of thought and life. The European
Christian world, impinging on Africa and Asia as well as the
Americas, took on new dimensions. The conciliar movement
had not been successful in removing the potentialities of
schism and expansion took place amid wars of religion. In
time, both Roman Catholicism and Protestantism, in part
accommodating to the new nationalism, began a remarkable
missionary expansion which made Christianity for the first
time in its history in fact world-wide.

The problem of the relation between Christianity and
culture still remains. Indeed, it is the most fundamental
issue concerning the place of religion in education today.
If Christian faith were without reason, or a Biblical literalism, it could make few if any claims on knowledge. That
Christianity has an intellectualism of its own is to be seen
from history. In present circumstances, the question is not
whether Christianity will be the only point of view represented in American public education: it is whether religion
will be represented at all! There are, of course, new factors
to be considered today which were not present in the medieval period: Protestantism, the Enlightenment and modern totalitarianism. Discussion of the relation of religion
and culture need not be limited to one confession; Judaism
as well as Christianity should be included. Curriculum would
be enriched and teaching strengthened by acceptance of
Dawson's basic thesis:

Behind the existing unity of Western culture we have the older unity of Christian culture which is the historic basis of our civilization. For more than a thousand years from the conversion of the Roman Empire down to the Reformation the peoples of Europe were fully conscious of their membership in the great Christian society and accepted the Christian faith and the Christian moral law as the ultimate bond of social unity and the spiritual basis of their way of life. Even after the unity of Christendom had been broken by the Reformation, the tradition of Christian culture still survived in the culture and institutions of the different European peoples. . . .

Consequently anyone who wishes to understand our own culture as it exists today cannot dispense with the study of Christian culture, whether he is a Christian or not. Indeed, in some ways this study is more necessary for the secularist than for the Christian.[21]

The strictly secular view of education that understands man as the beginning and end of his own life has now become impoverished. It has regarded human existence as a problem to be solved by man himself as he fights against nature, ignorance and the overbearing traditions of the past. Education has been conceived as an expression of man's faith in himself as the highest possibility, with power to master both matter and the irrational. Such faith has been challenged quite apart from religious criticism. Rush Welter has written:

Whether the pedagogical techniques employed are to be "progressive" or "conservative" they seem likely to eventuate in democratic pieties, and democratic pieties are hardly a solution for democratic problems. . . . Not only is the idea of informal political education likely to help dignify the calculated manipulation of public opinion by labeling it free competition in ideas; but any reaffirmation of the belief in education is likely to sanction unintelligent methods of dealing with na-

tional problems by making it seem that our only need is to do
the job we have always tried to do, but better. The preservation
of American democratic institutions depends upon the reality,
not the mythology, of democratic education.[22]

Existence would be much simpler if human beings knowing
the good, then proceeded to do it. But the person is not
simply reason or mind. He is impulse, intention and imagination. Knowing the good, he often ignores it.

Theism has a deeper sense of evil than non-religious views.
Judaism and Christianity refuse all belief in self-messianism.
Their hope is based on an ultimate good beyond all human
achievement which is not to be confused with it, namely,
the righteousness of God. On historical grounds, this view
has a legitimate place in teaching! Does trust in the grace
of God destroy human freedom? Christians have been clear
that it does not. The demand for moral sensitivity is not
made in the name of a blind or impersonal universe. The
ethical imperative is from a personal "Thou," outgoing and
self-giving. Education is the opportunity to realize values.
It is not simply an end in itself, but looks toward the
creative use of human potentialities. For Christians, it does
not have only a this-worldly significance, but contributes
to the growth of persons who have an eternal destiny.

"We hold these truths to be self-evident," wrote the
founders of the North American Republic. Man is endowed
by his Creator with inalienable rights—life, liberty and the
pursuit of happiness. Yet these rights have not seemed self-
evident, much less God-given to all men in the twentieth
century. Their reaffirmation requires that we probe the
deepest sensitivities of the human person in view of the
most abiding meanings and possibilities. What a man believes to be the truth determines significantly how he treats
both himself and others. Truth and freedom have an in-
timate relation to each other. The fact is that human rights

become most meaningful when they are understood in relation to the Providence of God, as the founders of the American Republic knew. We cannot afford to base respect for persons on any easy optimism about human goodness or history. Guardini judged correctly that modern man has come to the end of an era. New positive religious bases must be found for a creative intellectualism and humanism. The Founding Fathers would not have been satisfied with the situation described by Bernard Iddings Bell's telling remark: "As the American school system is now conducted, more and more conducted, there is no such thing as religious liberty in American education. There is only liberty to be unreligious." [23]

NOTES

1. Romano Guardini, *The End of the Modern World* (New York: Sheed and Ward, 1956).
2. T. S. Eliot, *The Idea of a Christian Society* (New York: Harcourt, 1940).
3. Christopher Dawson, *Education and the Crisis of Christian Culture* (Chicago: Regnery, 1949).
4. Reinhold Niebuhr, *The Nature and Destiny of Man* (New York: Scribner, 1949).
5. Will Herberg, *Protestant, Catholic, Jew: An Essay in American Religious Sociology* (New York: Doubleday, 1956).
6. Joseph Costanzo, *This Nation Under God* (New York: Herder, 1964), p. 91.
7. *Ibid.*, 89ff.
8. Everson v. Board of Education, 330 U.S. 1, pp. 23–24 (1947).
9. McCollum v. Board of Education, 333 U.S. 203 at 236 (1948).
10. Christopher Dawson, *The Crisis of Western Education* (New York: Sheed and Ward, 1961), pp. 119, 121.
11. *Ibid.*, p. 131.
12. *Ibid.*, p. 138.
13. Niels C. Nielsen, Jr., "Analogy as a Principle of Theological Method, Historically Considered," *The Heritage of Christian Thought*, ed. Robert E. Cushman and Egil Grislis (New York: Harper, 1965).
14. Hans Lietzmann, *Geschichte der Alten Kirche* (Berlin: de Gruyter, 1961), II, 297ff.

15. Hugo Rahner, *Kirche und Staat im Frühen Christentum* (Munich: Kösel, 1961).

16. Costanzo, *op. cit.*, p. 139.

17. Charles Norris Cochrane, *Christianity and Classical Culture* (New York: Oxford University Press, 1957), pp. 359ff.

18. Paul Tillich, *op. cit.*, III (1963), p. 250.

19. *Cambridge Medieval History*, XX, p. 529. Cited by Costanzo, *op. cit.*, p. 139.

20. Jacques Maritain, *True Humanism* (New York: Scribner, 1938).

21. Dawson, *op. cit.*, p. 136.

22. Rush Welter, *Popular Education and Democratic Thought in America* (New York: Columbia University Press, 1962), pp. 334–335.

23. Bernard Iddings Bell, *Crisis in Education* (New York: McGraw-Hill, 1949), p. 222.

8

The Problem of Confessional Differences

Is not any withdrawal of faith from education more than compensated for by the increased participation in institutional religion in the United States since the end of the Second World War? Church membership and attendance have grown so large that they now appear to be approaching a maximum. A majority of the people of the United States have some "voluntary" religious affiliation.[1] By contrast, Europe with its tradition of state support for institutional religion, has experienced no comparable "revival of religion." Has the new popular interest in religion brought increased understanding or increased commitment to the life of prayer and devotion? Asked in opinion polls whether religion really influences their lives, the majority of citizens answered negatively. Queried about the most elementary facts of religion, a large part of the population showed unmistakable ignorance.[2] Yet it is in style to be religious. As Will Herberg has pointed out, without the union of church and state, there is indeed a "national religion" in the United States.[3] It is found in the socially established practice to belong to one of the three major religious groups—Protestant, Catholic or Jewish.

In his *Protestant, Catholic, Jew,* Herberg attempts to explain the sociological role of these three parties in American life. Protestantism alone is no longer the only respectable position! Roman Catholicism and Judaism are acknowledged as well. Actually, all three of the "religions" have assured social status. For any serious religious view, the problem arises from the fact that the context of their acceptance is often that of secularism. Some 87 percent of Americans questioned in a public opinion poll answered that they hold belief in God as absolutely certain; 10 percent more are "fairly sure." [4] The overwhelming majority hold this conviction in the Hebrew or Christian tradition. About 83 percent of persons questioned described the Bible as in some sense the revealed Word of God. Yet 40 percent confessed they hardly ever or never read it. Sociological studies have explained more carefully than public opinion polls why personal faith does not affect individual life as deeply as the spread of institutional religion might suggest. In spite of outstanding differences between the confessions in the United States, religion has taken its own particular sociological patterns which in measure transcend denominational lines. The Hebrew-Christian view of life, its universalism as well as its prophetic insight, is threatened by the particularism of three "national religions." All responsible parties, Herberg believes, must seek to avoid this development. Practically the "state religion" is well patronized in its three forms. Yet this does not necessarily signify a vital dynamic, either personal or social. The lack of power in life is too often joined very simply with a lack of information if not obscurantism!

How effective are the educational strategies of organized religion? This is a question which is being asked more often than before by responsible leadership in all major groups. There is general cooperation between the leading Protestant denominations, Episcopal, Baptist, Methodist, Presbyterian, Lutheran, Congregational and Disciples of Christ, in such activities as associations of churches. A non-fundamentalist consensus has been achieved. However, in religious education, each denomination, indeed each local parish, establishes its own center, conveying really little information! Protestantism has made the Sunday School, now often renamed the "Church School," its primary vehicle. Large buildings continue to be constructed for classroom use, but results in learning remain unimpressive. Teaching has been done largely by laymen without professional training. Only a minimum of content can be given in a brief period on Sunday morning. Other church activities throughout the week are more often of a social than an educational character.

Among Protestants, the continued widespread interest in religion owes much to the revivals and awakenings of the eighteenth and nineteenth centuries. Frontier piety shared the American dream of liberty and sense of manifest destiny. It was equalitarian, even democratic, and by and large unsacramental. These traditions are now being challenged from within the Protestant community as well as from without.[5] Responsible leadership in the major denominations is prepared to take theological as well as ecumenical questions with all seriousness. Nor is the Protestant situation as sectarian as it first appears to be. Basically, Protestant denominations can be classified into a few families—Lutheran, Anglican, Presbyterian, Congregational, Methodist, Baptist and Disciples of Christ. The majority of Protestants belong to one of these groups and share common activities. The "revival of religion" has offered a wonderful opportunity for growth and deepened insight. It is an open question as to whether leadership has provided an educational opportunity equal to the needs of the time.

The Roman Catholic Church has developed its own parochial school system in the United States. This large effort has been made possible through the discipline and the sacrifice of its teaching brothers and sisters. Although school enrollments continue to increase, the number of persons volunteering for the teaching orders remain virtually the same. More lay teachers must be employed. The question is raised increasingly, as to how Church resources of funds and personnel can best be employed.[6] The Roman Catholic strategy has been in effect to develop a sub-community. The question is not whether it will dissolve into the larger patterns of culture as much as Protestantism, but whether it can give leadership. Is there to be more than a power struggle between religious groups? Is the openness and tolerance now expressed by church leadership in the ecumenical movement to reach to individual communities? One may hope that besides caring for their own institutions, Roman Catholic authorities will be prepared to consider the total problem of religious education. An all-or-nothing approach is least possible in a pluralistic society.

The majority Supreme Court opinion in the Regents' Prayer case made reference to attempts to impose uniformity in England before the American Revolution.[7] Whatever their immediate relevance, it is important to note that the state-church controversy in Europe was fresh in the memory of the men who wrote the American Constitution. They desired to avoid it if at all possible. Separation of Church and state was intended as a guarantee against political manipulation of religious loyalties. Such abuse had been all too evident in England ever since the time of the Reformation and King Henry VIII. This secular ruler had once been given the title "Defender of the Faith" for his earlier rejection of Lutheranism. His revolt against the authority of the Pope was more for political and personal than religious reasons. Following his death, a more self-consciously Protestant party came to power. The religion of the realm, as much as before, was determined by the monarch. Mary I attempted to restore Roman Catholicism. Following her reign, Elizabeth re-established Anglicanism and opposed Protestant sectarian controversy.

In time, Calvinism reappeared under Cromwell. It was a Presbyterian majority in Parliament which voted to restore the throne following his death. Nonetheless, the returning monarch brought back Anglicanism in force! In the end, Englishmen were convinced that religion ought not to change with the monarch. A man's inner conviction should be his own. Although establishment remained, a wider diversity of belief was accepted among Protestants. The ideas of such an advocate of tolerance as John Locke significantly influenced the American Revolution; still it is important to remember that Locke was throughout his life a devout churchman. Separation of church and state in the United States was not an attempt to secularize the common life, but to avoid forcing religion on anyone. Leaders such as Jefferson and Madison observed that intolerance is in fact a detriment to religion. The Enlightenment conviction made common cause with the Anabaptist tenet of freedom of conscience. Calvinists, on their own premises, advocated independence for the church, especially when they were in the minority.[8] Tolerance did not bespeak secularism, but the opposite—an intensification of religious loyalty in individual concern. In no major instance did it imply a relativistic or indifferentist view of religious truth.

Marty has explained the situation in the United States as follows: The writers of the Constitution abandoned the policy which had existed in Christendom ever since the first Christian Emperor, Constantine. It was he who began state support for religious undertakings. This pattern, which also characterized earlier paganisms, continued until the Enlightenment. It was as much Post-Reformation Protestant as Roman Catholic. The First Amendment, in effect, rejected the Constantinian settlement. The proof of the correctness of such action is a practical one: religion flourished. The institutional life of all religious groups has been large and vital under the separation of church and state in the United States. An educational strategy which envisages a return to the Constantinian policy ought to be rejected. The Supreme Court has attempted to distinguish between teaching and worship activities. If the claim for religion in the school is authentically educational, it should have a fair and open hearing. Significant confessional differences ought not to be ignored; the problem is how can they be acknowledged without surrender of the integrity of public education.

Can the ecumenical movement make any contribution? If ecumenical interest spreads greater understanding among Christians, the parochial school will profit from a more favorable atmosphere of life and work without losing its identity. New points of view are emerging which will eventually reach out to every level of life and work. The possibilities of parochial education need to be appraised against the whole background of renewal in the Roman Catholic Church as the result of the Second Vatican Council. Protestants cannot expect to see their fruition as long as they refuse to recognize the relevance of religion to public education and simply reaffirm the old phrase, "a wall of separation," as the solution to all problems. As Robert Hutchins, formerly Chancellor of the University of Chicago, has pointed out, walls do not solve issues! Equally uncritical is the opinion that the public schools are implicitly anti-religious.

"Ecumenical" means universal or catholic in the most inclusive sense. The movement which bears its name is without doubt the most important modern development in the life of Christendom. It does not look for compromise but new understanding. In this spirit, a wide range of problems are now being reconsidered in relation to contemporary issues and needs, problems which transcend denominational divisions. Roman Catholic appreciation for

Protestant modes of thought is being enriched by contacts at the top levels of leadership. Protestant observers have had an especially honored and recognized place at the Second Vatican Council. They are not limiting themselves to exclusive concern for the Bible, but have a new interest in questions of Christian history and tradition. Can Christian unity now be restored in the face of contemporary needs and problems? No responsible party expects such a development in the immediate future. There is no illusion that differences are anything but real and deep. Yet there can be greatly increased mutual understanding.

A new concern for Christian unity began among Protestants and Orthodox in the first part of this century.[9] The Roman Catholic Church which had its unity under the Pope was not immediately involved. The remainder of Christians were seriously divided among themselves. Nowhere was this more evident than in foreign missionary efforts. The World Missionary Conference, held in Edinburgh in 1910, brought this fact into focus and led to continuing organization in two major areas, Life and Work and Faith and Order. Conferences held on these two themes between the two world wars led to deepening concern across Protestant denominational lines, as well as to fresh contact between Europe and the United States. The World Council of Churches gave more lasting expression to Protestant and Orthodox cooperation. Planned before the Second World War, its first assembly was held in Amsterdam in 1948. The so-called new churches of Africa and Asia, founded by the missionary movements in the eighteenth and nineteenth centuries but subsequently independent, are also included. The World Council of Churches is in no sense a central authority, but a group of cooperating denominations representing churches from many different nations. Roman Catholic recognition of the importance of the growing ecumenical consciousness among Protestant and Orthodox Christians has led to a new situation in Christendom. Roman Catholic observers have been sent to World Council of Churches meetings.

The Roman Catholic Church did not participate directly in the Protestant and Orthodox movements for reunion, although it did maintain an interest in Christian unity. The dramatic action of Pope John XXIII in convening the Second Vatican Council, in effect, was a call to transcend old barriers of distrust and ill will. The Council is, of course, a Roman Catholic one; Protestants and Orthodox are only observers. Nevertheless, it has shown remarkable openness with its goals of renewal and reform. Ever since the Reformation, European Christians had often been defensively oriented as well as divided. A desperate fratricidal struggle between Christians, typified by the wars of religion, had followed the destruction of the medieval unity of Christendom. Tolerance was established in spite of continuing disagreement and hostility, primarily on secular grounds. Can a common cause be found again among Christians? Pope John XXIII and his successor, Pope Paul VI, have recognized that old formulations stand in need of fresh expression if they are to be relevant as against modern unbelief. In the face of common threats, Christians have rediscovered a common past. Post-Reformation polemics no longer seem relevant to either Protestants or Roman Catholics in Western Europe. There is a widespread recognition that Christian renewal is at the heart of any attempt to give our culture depth of insight and integrity in the face of modern nihilism.

The ecumenical movement has already brought a remarkable renewal of inner vitality to institutional religion. It is clear that Christians are not facing new developments simply defensively or negatively. The ecumenical movement is not a continuation of modernism—an attempt to bring religion up to date. Instead, the Christian consciousness is drawing on its own large and deep intellectual heritage with insights which by their very nature transcend old polemics. Roman Catholics and Protestants, whose churches had engaged in centuries of apologetics against each other, were together in concentration camps and even on the same gallows during the Nazi period.[10] Perhaps even more important, the rediscovery of Biblical modes of thought and interpretation through new scholarship has given fresh life to both Roman Catholic and Protestant theology. As never before, the Bible has become a place of meeting for Roman Catholics and Protestants in a common faith. To be sure, dogmatic differences remain, but are increasingly accepted in a new spirit. Roman Catholic leaders no longer speak of Protestants as heretics, but as separated brethren. The hierarchy is encouraging a new attitude toward the Jews as well. The dramatic good will of Pope John XXIII continues to challenge the old clichés of non-Roman Catholics.

It is important to recognize that the new ecumenical discussion has a different background in the United States than in Europe. The Protestant tradition is more one of the free churches, rather than the older confessions of the Reformation. Disestablishment has brought larger Protestant denominational diversity. The variety of organizational structures presents different problems than in Europe where there are not as many major religious groups. Roman Catholicism in the United States is young and vigorous, with large lay participation. Piety remains vital among the working classes, a group which is largely lost to the churches in much of Europe. Rather than being directed into Marxist revolt, social protest has taken more Christian forms, both Roman Catholic and Protestant. Until the Second Vatican Council, there was a largely defensive attitude between the major religious bodies at the theological level. Most important, the confessions were not drawn together as much as in Europe through persecution by the totalitarian state. What can the ecumenical movement mean in the heterogeneous American scene? Can it bring any insight to the educational problems which seem to counter efforts of leadership on both sides toward mutual understanding?

Even more than in Europe, re-evaluation is required within the confessions themselves. Experienced observers of religion in the United States continue to ask whether interconfessional relations—in particular at the local level—can develop deeper than just superficial good will.[11] What will result if American Christians abandon their defensive attitudes and develop a deeper appreciation for each other's ideas? One must be warned against expecting too much in immediate change. There are abiding barriers as well as differences of conviction; the common temptation is to refute persons who disagree with us rather than to listen to them and understand what they are saying. In the United States, the ecumenical movement could mean that Christians become less sectarian in education in recognition of common needs and interests. Can Roman Catholics and Protestants by mutual understanding arrive at a more creative solution of the problem of teaching about religion—one appropriate to the dynamic pluralistic culture in which they live? The Second Vatican Council has begun a process whose end cannot yet be envisaged. In time, cooperation may reach to education. It is not utopian to point out that it offers the only real alternative for a more positive role for religion in the face of a self-conscious secularism.

NOTES

1. Will Herberg, *Protestant, Catholic, Jew: An Essay in American Religious Sociology* (New York: Doubleday, 1956), pp. 59–61.
2. *Ibid.*, pp. 85f.
3. *Ibid.*, p. 262.
4. *Ibid.*, p. 235.
5. A. Roy Eckardt, *The Surge of Piety in America* (New York: Association Press, 1958).

6. Robert T. Francoeur, "The Price We Pay," *Commonweal*, Vol. 79, No. 18 (January 31, 1964), pp. 538f.

7. Ralph Barton Perry, *Puritanism and Democracy* (New York: Vanguard Press, 1944), pp. 62ff.

8. Leo Pfeffer, *Creeds in Competition: A Creative Force in American Culture* (New York: Harper, 1958), pp. 27–28.

9. Ruth Rouse and Stephen Charles Neill, eds., *A History of the Ecumenical Movement, 1517–1948* (London: SPCK, 1954).

10. Heinrich Hermelink, *Kirche im Kampf* (Tübingen: Leins, 1950).

11. Reinhold Niebuhr, *Essays in Applied Christianity* (New York: Meridian, 1959). "The acrimonious relations between Catholics and Protestants in this country are scandalous. If two forms of the Christian faith, though they recognize a common Lord, cannot achieve a little more charity in their relations to each other, they have no right to speak to the world or claim to have any balm for the world's hatreds and mistrusts" (p. 220).

9

Ecumenism and the Second Vatican Council

The Second Vatican Council has distinguished between ecumenicity in general and Roman Catholic ecumenical teaching.[1] The latter presupposes that the fullness of all Christian truth and life is implicit in the Roman Catholic Church. What can be said about the role of other groups of professed Christians who do not share this premise? There has been discussion in the Council as to whether their denominations should be described as "religious communities" or "churches." The opinions of Protestant and Orthodox observers have been heard and respected, although they have not participated directly in the deliberations of the Council. Pope John, in calling the assembly of bishops, stated explicitly that he wished no new dogmatic definitions which would further separate Christians.[2] The presence of the observers in the Aula of St. Peter's has been symbolic of a consciousness among the Fathers of the Council of the importance of the "separated brethren." Pastor Max Lackmann, an observer for the "Association for Protestant-Catholic Reunion" and who was imprisoned at Dachau with Roman Catholic clergy in the Nazi period, speaks of John

XXIII as the first ecumenical pope.[3] It can hardly be denied that the change in the ethos of interconfessional relations has been spectacular— as Cardinal König has remarked, more than either Roman Catholics or Protestants had expected. For many Protestants, Vatican II has meant the end of the Counter Reformation.

Roman Catholic scholars continue to re-examine what can be said from their own tradition. Father Bernard Lambert, O.P., is a responsible theologian who stays well within the bounds of what is acceptable in his communion; nonetheless, he is able to use a wide variety of material from non-Roman Catholic studies in his two-volume work, *The Ecumenical Problem*.[4] One important issue now open to full and frank discussion, he reports, is the non-theological factors in the division of Christendom. Father Lambert argues from the theological premise that the Roman Catholic Church is not absolutely self-contained in isolation, although reunion with other Christians would add nothing to its essential perfection. He is explicit in his view that following the Reformation, certain resources of Christian faith and life were developed more in non-Roman Catholic milieux than in his own communion. He emphasizes especially the contribution of Protestantism to Biblical study as well as the Eastern Orthodox sense of eschatology.

Still at the level of non-theological factors, the new ecumenical interest asks how much a particular nationality, land, geography or culture, American or European, Occidental or Oriental, is reflected in particular religious communities. Of course, Christianity is in principle transcultural, international and universal, but not simply so. It has concrete historical form as an expression of incarnation. Father Lambert raises the particularly important problem of Christianity's relation to Africa and Asia. Are we to expect these continents to accept all European social divisions? What sort of cultural synthesis is relevant? How much is the

Reformation just a Western, European phenomenon, as some
Japanese Christians have wished to regard it?

It may well be that non-theological factors can be discussed more easily than others. They are nevertheless important, and recognition of their presence can reduce
confusion. Lambert stresses that Christianity is a religion
which expresses itself in particular cultures. Eastern Orthodox Christianity has been significantly bound up with Greek
civilization; Roman Catholicism and in a measure Protestantism have been identified, on the other hand, with the
Latin West. Lambert comments that Eastern Orthodox
Christians regard their church as embodying the pattern to
which other Christians must return in reunion. They tend
at times to regard both Roman Catholicism and Protestantism as belonging to a common Western family, influenced by
Augustine as they are not. To be sure, as Protestant scholars
discovered in post-Reformation dialogue, the Eastern Church
is catholic, sacramental and not just Biblicist.

Lambert considers the sociological differences between
"church" and "sectarian" types of orientation. This distinction is of special importance in dealing with Protestantism.
Ecumenical discussion runs the danger of dealing in theological stereotypes if it ignores this important polarity. If
there is to be a dialogue at responsible levels with Protestants, Roman Catholic scholarship must attempt to understand Protestantism in part on its own terms. Its claims may
be approached phenomenologically in description as well
as on theological grounds. Most important is the fact that
Protestant low church groups—now the majority in the
United States—do not regard institutional religion as a
means of grace; although their church is for them a spiritual
community, its institutional role does not carry theological
sanctions. This fact explains in part the often ambiguous
attitudes toward religion in education among low church
Protestant groups. Reinhold Niebuhr has warned that the

"Protestant heritage disintegrates into secularism much more easily than Catholicism does." [5] And yet, Reformation Protestantism, like Roman Catholicism and Orthodoxy, has theological perspectives for institutional life. Practically, the differences with the free churches are not as large as they at first appear; responsible leadership in the major denominations recognizes responsibility for community life. Yet diverse traditions will require considerable time for rapprochement in discussion.

As Lambert points out, there is integration and disintegration in institutional life in spite of theologies. A variety of strategies are needed. Of course, it is a mistake to suppose that individual conviction is enough to give religion a place in education. Institutional problems remain. Increasingly, integration takes place in other areas besides religion today. At the sociological level, the ecumenical movement is a recognition of the need for regrouping in the face of competing forces. The theological problem, by contrast, remains one of wholeness, the healing and renewal of Christendom. The two are not the same but related. Contact can bring either opposition or accommodation. The unhappy fact is that among Christians the former rather than the latter often has appeared most readily. The alternative to irresponsible accommodation is ecumenical dialogue with mutual respect for truth and freedom.

Lambert is correct in saying that a sort of "moral rearmament," not in the sense of indifferentism much less a lowest common denominator, is prerequisite to ecumenical exchange. Assuredly, this is needed in education as it is related to religion as much as in any area. The first reaction to another Christian confession, more often than not, is defensive, but it need not remain so. Open discussion does not mean that questions of cult or tradition are to be ruled out, but taken with new seriousness and importance. Of course, Roman Catholic study cannot afford to ignore the ecumenical and theological renewal in Protestantism; the literature must be available and open to study. The cultural isolation which separated religious communities in the past is breaking down in a new type of pluralism. The Vatican Council has envisaged fresh openness to the world and its needs as well as to what is being said by different groups of Christians. In such circumstances, it would be mistaken to suppose that Christianity demands uniformity of culture. Are the mistakes of Greek-Latin relations to be repeated in another guise in the expanding world outlook today as Africa and Asia have contact with Christian teaching? Cultural change brings danger as well as the possibility of re-evaluation and new synthesis. One cannot expect all Roman Catholics or Protestants to respond at once in an ecumenical spirit, in education. Yet it is not too much to say that simple isolation with its "siege mentality" is breaking down.

The Dutch Jesuit and sociologist Harry Hoefnagels has pointed out discerningly the changed social circumstances and attitudes which are emerging. Modern society has developed its own characteristic forms of secular life; in many countries, Christians are now a minority.[6] The churches are compelled to tolerance and ecumenicity. The older attempt to establish a Christian milieu in cooperation with the state was in many respects a dubious one. Royalty not only took an interest in religion; it also tried to control it. The attempt to perpetuate "milieu Christianity" through control of communication and education with the development of closed sub-groups, has been sharply criticized by Carl Amery in Germany.[7] Hoefnagels does not accept Amery's negative judgments completely. As a sociologist, he recognizes that the social context in which religion is practiced is of continuing importance. More significant, however, than any struggle for accepted social patterns, he believes, is free loyalty to religious truth through individual responsibility.

The frequently mentioned example is the case of the Roman Catholic Breton peasant who moves to Paris and gives up the practice of his faith in conformity with his new working-class urban environment. More than a return to the past is necessary in dealing with de-Christianization. It is not possible simply to enforce the full limits of an earlier segregation in a mixed modern community. That a pluralistic society embodies a variety of points of view in competition is not necessarily evil! Free and open ecumenical discussion among Christians as well as dialogue in tolerance with other world views is required.

Roman Catholic ecumenicists call attention to the claim that all baptized Christians belong to the mystical body of Christ. Cardinal Bea, head of the Secretariat for Christian Unity, has repeatedly emphasized the presence of this idea in recent papal encyclicals.[8] Other than pastoral issues are at stake. The problem is not just theological but sociological: the confessionalism which isolates one Christian community from another is not as effective as before. Christians are required to know and consider alternatives, not just in terms of "black and white" any more than through indifferentism or extreme individualism which derogate history and tradition. The deliberations of the Second Vatican Council have shown—for all the world to see—that there is diversity in Roman Catholic thought as well as outstanding differences with Protestant and Eastern Orthodox Christians. The Roman Catholic Church is not just an effective administrative organization but a living community with internal dialogue.

An important chapter in Cardinal Bea's widely circulated book, *The Unity of Christians,* is entitled "Academic Research and Teaching in the Service of the Unity of Christians." [9] More than a quarter of a century ago while he was head of the Pontifical Biblical Institute in Rome, Cardinal Bea recounts, he was invited to attend a New Testament Congress at the University of Göttingen in Germany. Inasmuch as the invitation came somewhat unexpectedly, he consulted with Pope Pius XI, who advised him to attend. Cardinal Bea's experience was an encouraging one which showed him what a wide range of possibilities are actually open. Of course, Roman Catholic scholars now participate with Protestants and Jews in such meetings. Cardinal Bea endorses joint work in philosophy and the history of philosophy with Protestants; it has the value of contributing to an understanding of the intellectual background of theological expression. He includes the history of dogma and even the study of dogma itself as areas of cooperation. Biblical research is not to be isolated confessionally any more than Church history. Both have their necessary data. Finally, study of natural law, literature, art history as well as natural science should be common concerns; they can be undertaken ecumenically with mutual enhancement as well as new insight. While Cardinal Bea's work has been conducted at the most advanced levels, his ecumenical concern has great relevance for education in general.

Serious Roman Catholic self-criticism has come from such ecumenical theologians as the Swiss, Hans Küng.[10] Küng, whose books have carried the endorsement of leading members of the hierarchy, does not stand alone in criticizing a too "churchly" view which destroys the "worldly" relevance of Christian faith. The Church must guard against isolation on the one hand and modernism on the other. Pope John's intention in calling the Second Vatican Council, he points out, was one of reform, not restoration or revolution. Has the Council come too soon? Küng asks. Are Roman Catholics ready for the new ecumenical spirit? The Roman Catholic-Protestant dialogue, Küng believes, has been too long delayed. For nearly a generation following the Reformation, there was serious consideration of reunion on both sides. Then, confessional intransigence became dominant in the wars of religion. Not alone civil tolerance but the expansion of European civilization with the discovery of the Americas and fresh routes to Asia, brought a new task of dialogue. Stereotypes of schism and heresy are all too easily barriers to reform as well as to reunion. Küng argues that the demand for the reform of the Church is not exclusively Protestant. Indeed, it had monumental expression in the Middle Ages through the work of the great monastic movements and their struggle against worldliness and secularism. Father Yves Congar's distinction between a true and false reformation remains fundamental for the Roman Catholic point of view.[11] Reformation ought not to have meant the rejection of the structures of the Church. In the modern world, it must proceed from a new sense of mission and tolerance, not a renewed juridical emphasis.

Küng, loyal to his own tradition, believes that the Protestant Reformers were wrong in rejecting the Roman Catholic priesthood and teaching office. Yet he argues that the Roman Catholic Church in the early sixteenth century did not embody the Christian message and truth clearly enough; in short, it was in need of reform. When the Conciliar movement failed to effect the needed change, the Reformation and Counter Reformation were the unhappy consequences. Küng refers to the goal set by Pope John XXIII in calling the Second Vatican Council: the Roman Catholic Church should embody the Christian faith so completely that the separated brethren and the world will be attracted to it. In interpreting this goal, Küng develops an interesting theory of representation. The Council, like the Church, is an assembly of the faithful which comes together primarily at the call of God. Its task is to speak for the whole Church. If the Council is really representative, it cannot ignore the separated brethren. These, too, belong to the mystical body of Christ and it must seek to express whatever is true in their faith. Truth comes in obedience to the Gospel; the Council like the Church needs to be faithful to the call of God.

Küng's theory of representation is a criticism of all self-absolutizing tendencies. He cites the remark of the Swiss Protestant theologian, Karl Barth, that the Protestant cannot hear the voice of the Good Shepherd, Christ, in the Roman Catholic Church. Should not the Roman Catholic Church embody Christ's word so clearly that even Protestants can hear it? Küng concludes.

There is a very sound basis in Roman Catholic theology for ecumenical conviction. Professor Fries of the University of Munich, a very responsible but ecumenically-minded Roman Catholic theologian, points out that Roman Catholics and Protestants agree in the belief that the Church as the community of the faithful is sent from God.[12] Its source is in divine grace and revelation. Roman Catholics and Protestants came a long way together in Christian history and share the heritage of nearly fifteen centuries. In view of the present ecumenical development, Fries argues, Roman Catholics should regard Protestantism as a call to renewal, even though not accepting its claim fully. It ought not to be dismissed simply as untrue under the charge of heresy. Fries stresses that the Second Vatican Council represents the beginning of a new phase of dialogue between the different Christian confessions. Ecumenicism is no longer limited to a particular party of theologians; it is officially the interest of the Roman Catholic Church. Fries even suggests that the variety of views represented by the different confessions are the modern counterpart of the pre-Reformation theological schools: Augustinian, Thomistic and Scotist. However this may be, there has been a growing realization on both sides that theology ought not to be conducted as monologue or self-justification.

Roman Catholic ecumenicists criticize Protestantism on the grounds that it too often seeks to reduce the whole to the particular in a one-sided emphasis on faith, grace and scripture alone. However, they recognize as well that Protestants find major difficulties in Roman Catholic ecclesiology especially as regards hierarchy and tradition. They urge that Protestants ought to welcome new Roman Catholic attempts to justify their Church's position in Biblical terms rather than invoking its jurisdictional powers. Fries believes that in fact Protestantism has had the positive effect of intensifying the Roman Catholic sense of "Heilsgeschichte," or the history of salvation. Ecumenicity does not mean that one gives up his own conviction or the faith of his communion; rather, both are informed in dialogue. This was not possible in an older era of polemics and political struggle.

Only time alone will tell whether the present ecumenical interest will lead to a new dynamic community relation between Christians. It can hardly be denied that there has been growing disappointment on the part of many Protestant observers, as their hopes for the Second Vatican Council have not been fully realized.[13] The schema on the Church seems to them to have been too much weakened by conservative interpolations. The decree on religious liberty was held over until another session by papal initiative. Yet short-term accomplishments must be judged against longer prospects. One must ask what was expected? Was the Roman Catholic Church to make itself just another denomination, much less to renounce jurisdiction? Through its episcopal structures it has conveyed ecumenism even to its members who have accepted the idea reluctantly, more than has often been the case in Protestantism. Before the Council, responsible Protestant leadership hoped most of all for increased religious freedom in Spain and South America. There are now signs of new tolerance in these areas. Another important field where ecumenical intentions will be tested in concrete decisions of tolerance and cooperation or intolerance and intransigence is education. If the spirit of the Second Vatican Council can bring real freedom as against communalism, a new relation will have been effected.[14]

NOTES

1. *Decretum de Oecumenismo* (Freiburg: Herder, 1965), p. 150.
2. Hans Küng, *Kirche im Konzil* (Freiburg: Herder, 1963), p. 19. Cf. also Küng's *The Council in Action* (New York: Sheed and Ward, 1963).
3. Max Lackmann, *Mit evangelischen Augen, Beobachtungen eines Lutheraners auf dem Zweiten Vatikanischen Konzil* (Graz: Styria, 1964), II, p. 9.
4. Bernard Lambert, *Das ökumenische Problem* (Freiburg: Herder, 1964).
5. Cf. Reinhold Niebuhr, *Essays in Applied Christianity* (New York: Meridian, 1959).
6. Harry Hoefnagels, *Kirche in Veränderten Welt* (Essen: Driewer, 1964), pp. 35ff.
7. Carl Amery, *Die Kapitulation oder Deutscher Katholizismus heute* (Reinbek bei Hamburg: Rowohlt, 1963).
8. Augustin Cardinal Bea, *Die Einheit der Christen* (Freiburg: Herder, 1963), p. 24. Cf. also Bea's *Unity in Freedom* (New York: Harper, 1964).
9. *Ibid.*, pp. 63ff.
10. Hans Küng, *Konzil und Wiedervereinigung* (Vienna: Herder, 1960), pp. 8off. Cf. also Küng's *The Council, Reform and Reunion* (New York: Sheed and Ward, 1961).
11. Yves Congar, *Chrétiens désunis, principes d'un "oecuménisme" catholique* (Paris: Cerf, 1937).
12. Heinrich Fries, *Aspekte der Kirche* (Stuttgart: Schwabenverlag, 1963), pp. 153ff.
13. Cf., Herder *Correspondence* I, 57, 283–285.
14. Hans Küng, *Kirche im Konzil, op. cit.*

10

New Conditions and Common Problems

Protestants and Roman Catholics ought to agree to this much: The role of religion in public education cannot be determined by judicial review alone. It depends most of all on the initiative of responsible leaders in local communities—schools, churches and synagogues.[1] As in the case of the Supreme Court decision on desegregation, a minimum public consensus is needed if its ruling is to become the common will. Controversy can become so intense as to render its directives ineffective. Decisions on religion in the schools have evoked intense feeling because they have inevitably been directed against one or another competing view, not only in the classroom but in the community in general. There are Protestant as well as Roman Catholic and Jewish special interests which the Supreme Court has attempted to neutralize. The large majority of Protestants affirm a wall of separation with renewed intensity and defensiveness. Roman Catholic leadership is often fored to give first attention to its own institutions rather than any community effort. What can or should religious forces contribute to public education? At the top levels of leadership, there is clearly a larger common interest among Roman Catholics and Protestants. But, actually, the new ecumenical concern has only a limited outreach.

It is our thesis that religious institutions should support the integrity of teaching. It is they most of all who ought to insist that learning is not just practical, but intellectual and cultural. Immediate community needs are not to be derogated, but must be seen in a larger social and historical context. Religious influence is needed to help to restore a responsible set of values in education against pragmatism which is now largely rejected. It should stand as well for professional integrity and the freedom of the teacher. Is such influence possible; can it become effective? Partisan controversy can make religion even more irrelevant to teaching than ever before. At present, it is clear that religious differences have been a barrier in the way of a national educational policy. Opposition to any federal aid to parochial schools comes from a variety of groups, secular and religious. The question is not only whether such subsidy is constitutional, a matter to be decided finally by the courts. It is whether a whole range of problems—including the place of religion in public education—can be avoided by centering attention almost exclusively on the separation of church and state.

In the nineteenth century, American educational institutions, especially the colleges and universities, were predominately Protestant.[2] As Roman Catholics have grown in number, they have founded their own centers of higher learning. Although state-supported land-grant institutions were established early in the history of the nation, they did not immediately develop strength. In this century, they have recently come to enroll more than half of college and university students. Forecasts show that they will soon serve at least three-fourths of the persons enrolled in higher education. The influence of Protestant-sponsored institutions has declined, although some continue to rank among the best in the nation. Some schools have broken completely with their earlier religious ties; in others, the curriculum is increasingly secularized. Major re-evaluation is called for! It has become imperative for Protestantism to transcend a relatively narrow denominational base in a larger educational interest in religion as something more than sectarian. Roman Catholic educational undertakings in this country have had a much larger geographical spread than in Europe. However, its leaders are frank to admit that their efforts have not yet reached a level comparable with the best in Europe. A few Roman Catholic institutions—McCluskey finds about half a dozen universities and no more than two dozen colleges—rank as schools of high quality; others suffer from lack of resources.[3]

Look magazine once carried a report of the life of a nun, a teacher in a parochial school.[4] Her sacrifice and devotion to duty were depicted in all their strength and simplicity. The same issue of the magazine described the effect of television horror programs on young children. Scenes of murder, robbery and violence, psychologists have concluded, have a warping effect on immature minds. It seems, therefore, legitimate to ask the question: Why does American society allow full secular freedom to television programming with its often negative conditioning influence, but refuse to support parochial education? Roman Catholic leadership now faces greatly increased costs in the attempt to maintain its own parochial school system. More than two and one half billion dollars are now being expended annually. Such schools make a continuing contribution to good citizenship. Ought not a genuinely pluralistic society to encourage such schools on educational if not religious grounds?

In fact, an all-or-nothing approach, too often set in stereotypes in public discussion, gives little real help in solving immediate problems. Non-Catholics tend to view the issue only from the point of view of the separation of church and state. Roman Catholic leadership fears that its institutions will be discriminated against if federal subsidy is given only to public schools. Too often, Protestants continue in the role of giving advice to Roman Catholics without any particular proposal of their own for religious education. More than this, they expect Roman Catholics to give up their hard-won gains in the establishment of parochial schools even as public education is secularized, often to the extreme. Of course, the demand for the funds necessary for new buildings and scientific equipment as well as increased salaries for growing lay staffs, has put heavy strains upon resources in some geographical areas, more than in others.

The fundamental question is how parochial schools are to be treated fairly without favoritism or derogation as education continues to expand. A common Christian concern which would support religious interests in general and even in the end help to meet particular denominational needs, seems far away. If all Roman Catholic attention is given to parochial schools, one need not expect that the educational pattern in general will reflect Catholic principles. The public schools are not anti-religious, much less simply Protestant as is sometimes implied. No doubt, legal controversy about possible state aid for parochial schools will continue. Yet in principle it seems clear enough that the responsibility of religious leadership is a double one. On the one hand, schools which are committed to particular religious traditions are needed as much as before. They allow and strengthen the outreach of an explicit faith commitment into every area of knowledge; without them, religious instruction becomes too easily circumscribed. On the other hand, there is need for responsible recognition of the importance of religious ideas in all aspects of education, whether sponsored privately or by the state.

In fact, there is a large area of consensus among all major

parties concerning the separation of church and state. Financial support of the church by the state, practiced in various forms in Christendom since the time of Constantine, is recognized without question as unconstitutional. Does disestablishment mean that religious symbols and ideas have no place in the national life? Such a view would require new precedents for both theory and practice. Establishment can denote a variety of things. It means, initially, state subsidy for the building of churches and the salaries of clergy. Such aid, given to state churches in Christendom, has carried its own particular set of problems. It is a different polity than the free voluntary support characteristic of religious institutions in the United States. The constitutional guarantee of freedom of conscience has supported diversity in religious belief. Under it, the Roman Catholic and Jewish minorities became a working part of a nation which had been initially almost exclusively Protestant. By and large, disestablishment has been successful in keeping religious controversy out of public life. Roman Catholics, Protestants and Jews as well as non-believers all accept in principle the separation of church and state.

It is in the area of education that the consensus concerning church-state relations breaks down. Does freedom of conscience imply that all publicly supported education must be exclusively secular in character? The intellectual and cultural tradition which it must seek to convey has deep roots in the Hebrew-Christian legacy. Religious ideas and conviction have long contributed significantly to teaching and learning in Western Europe. Religious support for education is not an innovation. In the Middle Ages, as in the post-Reformation era, universities were founded under church sponsorship; much of the teaching was carried on by clergy. The first universities in the United States were conducted under religious auspices, which were largely Protestant. Common schools were established to train and inform the laity as well as to prepare clergy, in short, to insure a responsible citizenry for service in church and state. Morality and knowledge of God were understood to belong together. In the face of increased pluralism, religious instruction was abandoned in the public school. This was not the consequence of anticlericalism or an overt secularism. The dominant Protestant majority in effect "backed into it," without planning or foresight. In New York, for example, Governor Seward proposed to subsidize both Roman Catholic and Protestant private schools.[5] The Scotch Presbyterians supported his position. Public opinion, however, was on the side of the Free School Society, and its wish for a common school prevailed. The earlier church-home-school pattern broke down. Protestants could look to the public school only for general education; special religious training had to be given one day per week in the Sunday School. Roman Catholic parochial schools gave religion a larger place throughout the week. In the public school, common religious commitment continued to allow such practices as Bible reading and the recitation of the Lord's Prayer.

The traditions of the Constitution are appealed to as such usages are re-evaluated. Of course, it is not explicit about them. It is clear enough that government should not subsidize the worship of a particular church, but not that Christian ideas should be excluded from education. As Robert M. Healey has pointed out, Thomas Jefferson believed that the best way to encourage religion—in education as in all other areas—was to support freedom of conscience against compulsion.[6] He believed that religion has a positive, indeed a necessary place in the common life. Establishment—the dominant tradition throughout the larger part of the history of Christendom—too often placed it on the side of privilege or power. Freed from such abuse, religion would flourish. In the United States there was no official church; yet this did not mean that morality was to be separated from belief in God. The Christian ideas of creation, natural law and justice were all too evident in the dominant doctrines of the time. Their world-affirming ethos of the belief in freedom is not to be explained apart from religion. Yet a clear distinction was not made between the natural and supernatural, nor was the all-important question asked: When specifically Christian ideals and principles are not accepted in culture, what is to replace the devotion they evoke? It was supposed simply that Christianity "fell" by becoming institutionalized and joined to the state. A new individualism would repair the loss. Now it has become more clear that a society which does not accept the commandments of God tends to take on what Tillich has identified as the "demonic" dimensions in modern totalitarianism.

It is easy enough to criticize the support of the church by the state in a democratic society which has adequate resources for a diversity of institutional undertakings. In fact, the Constantinian acceptance of Christianity was only the beginning of a long readjustment in both church and state.[7] Religious leadership could not remain irresponsible, looking only for the end of the world. Rather, it had to seek out the relevance of eternal truth to all of the problems of the time. Sectarian polemic for the complete separation of religion from government too often forgets that political arrangements do matter. Some understanding with an existing regime, even a minimal one, can make life easier for Christians in the modern totalitarian state. In the United States, the question is not one of rapprochement between the church and state; pluralism has led to a diversity of religious parties. The question is rather whether religion has relevance for the content and quality of teaching and learning. One must appraise what principles are valid and then ask whether it is possible to overcome existent barriers in both politics and ecclesiology. The question of principle is whether it is really sound education to exclude all consideration of destiny, evil or ultimate meaning in pragmatic compromise. Of course, they can hardly be carried into the open by schoolmen unless a variety of religious parties are more willing to accept their responsible discussion without exerting a simply sectarian pressure. The massive fact of the Hebrew-Christian tradition remains; only the most one-sided view of the culture can ignore it.

Recourse to a doctrine of separation of church and state in an attempt to conceal the religious roots of Western civilization remains unsound simply from the point of view of learning. The basic question is how to appropriate the achievements of the past without being bound to them in an overbearing traditionalism. Of course, freedom of conscience means that each man's decisions are his own. Yet this need not imply that religion is a wholly private matter or without relevance to moral or social responsibility. The Hebrew-Christian tradition is emphatic that the world is God's creation and his commands are to be obeyed in all of life. The extreme sectarian view unwittingly supports secularism as individual Christians remain unconcerned about the problems of learning, interested only in the otherworldly salvation of their souls. Too often, Protestants have failed to appraise realistically the appalling vacuum in religious education brought about by such commitment. Too often, they are satisfied with a faith affirmation as the end rather than as the beginning of knowledge. The fundamentalist view like that of the modernist has little to say to culture; the alternative is one of uncritical rejection or acceptance. The paradox of the present situation is that Protestantism today has excellent intellectual leadership as well as theological renewal. The question is how such leadership can be effective if there is a continuing retreat from major sources of communication and competence in education.

Conrad Henry Moehlman in his *School and Church* published two decades ago, stated frankly that democracy and not Christianity is the religion of the American majority.[8] He proposed to limit religious education to the home and church. From the point of view of traditional theism, Moehlman's position is idolatrous; democracy is no substitute for belief in God. Practically, Moehlman failed to take note of the growing religious interest of the American people. No doubt, explicitly secularist opinion has become more self-conscious than before and its impact is not to be minimized. A larger effect, however, than any it has brought about has been accomplished by an irresponsible denominationalism. Full integration of the teaching of any one particular religious group with the public school curriculum is not possible in the face of pluralism. Granted that the situation is not ideal, is it hopeless? In short, must all religious ideas be excluded until there is full community consensus? Implicitly the schools will teach about religion; the real question is under what circumstances. Must teaching reduce to a lowest possible denominator, a common core to which no one can object? This is the central problem. Responsible leadership knows that such unanimity is hardly to be expected in any other field: science, history, literature or economics. If full agreement is necessary, no real options can be presented.

Recent Supreme Court decisions at first appear to require complete exclusion of consideration of religion apart from such agreement. Yet Justice Clark was careful to state that the separation of church and state need not be so interpreted.[9] That the church should not control the state is in the American tradition. That education should be completely without reference to religion is in fact an innovation. The question is not only one of legal precedent, but of the ethos of educational practice. Separated from the tradition of the high religions, common loyalties take the form of a national patriotic cult. In this case, ultimate loyalty is not really ignored, but transferred to the state, although without any overt fanaticism. One faith loyalty is excluded for another. But this is precisely what the Supreme Court has rejected, establishment of secularism as an alternative to the theism of the Protestant, Roman Catholic and Jewish confessions. The basic question is how the insights of their respective traditions are to be made relevant in a pluralistic society.

It is clear that teaching about religion in the public schools should not be a simply Protestant or Christian strategy. Special instruction in doctrine belongs to representatives of the churches in their own groups. Yet a background of understanding about what religion teaches and practices can be developed as part of general education. Consultation with leading scholars from the major confessions would be an important factor in teacher training and preparation of course material. Yet, in the end, subject matter must carry its own meaning. If the churches and synagogues were prepared to support a joint agency, advised but not controlled by religious leadership, the educational community could respond positively.[10] It can support an essentially intellectual interest in teaching about religion because it is not simply sectarian. At present, initiative has been reduced. Religously concerned persons ought not to ignore what is at stake. If Roman Catholic, Protestant and Jewish parties cannot make their concerns meaningful to education, the margin of irrelevance will increase rather than decrease!

The present ecumenical concern can serve as an encouragement to educational as well as religious leadership. It is to be hoped that new insights for teaching about religion will develop as representatives of major groups have increased contact with each other. Officially, Roman Catholicism has shown a larger interest in what the Protestant and Jewish parties think and teach. Of course, eclecticism is to be avoided. It is important not to equate the educational with the ecumenical problem, although the two are related. Some teaching about religion may be possible in spite of divisions. Roman Catholics will not achieve, in this century at least, all that they may wish for in parochial school education in the United States. If they cannot educate as widely as they had hoped, they may be required to turn to other strategies. To be sure, this development would be a second choice, but may yet become necessary. Protestant leadership has not made an all-out defense of prayer or Bible reading in the public school. It ought to say what it does and does not want and not let itself drift into an attempt to solve educational problems simply by affirming the separation of church and state. Protestants need to consider more earnestly the whole involvement of religion with culture, both in the past and in the present. Oversimplified faith claims that the Bible alone provides all the religious knowledge necessary for its reader become a covert anti-intellectualism.

One ought not to underestimate the practical barriers to such concern in view of the various demands made on the Protestant pastor, or for all that matters on the Roman Catholic parish administrator. Their responsibility too often is exclusively the defense of ecclesiastical interests. If the churches really wish their influence to be felt in the struggle of ideas, they must be willing to attempt to meet the new conditions of education. The school is first of all an agency of instruction with its own positive ethos. Public school officials have long developed defenses against sectarian pressures, which at the same time do not challenge religious agencies directly. Supreme Court decisions have strengthened rather than weakened the autonomy of educational agencies. Whatever develops from the suggestion that it is legitimate to "teach about" religion, remains largely for religious parties to decide. In fact, little can be accomplished short of serious self-criticism. Among Protestants, the educational ineffectiveness of the Sunday School is scandalous. Large sums of money continue to be spent on plants which are used only one day a week. The Jewish concern is often largely defensive, and ecumenical interest has yet to reach to popular levels of thought and practice in a large part of the Roman Catholic community. Yet the fact remains that no party can destroy the other! Should there not be a responsible dialogue between them in relation to education? The present ecumenical concern bespeaks the vitality and integrity of responsible religious leadership and cannot but have an effect on education. Although it will not solve all existing problems, it may yet make their discussion easier.

NOTES

1. *Religion and the Free Society* (New York: Fund for the Republic, 1958).
2. Stokes and Pfeffer, *op. cit.*, pp. 165–166.
3. Neil G. McCluskey, "A Changing Pattern," *Commonweal*, Vol. 79, No. 18 (January 31, 1964), pp. 507ff.
4. *Look*, vol. XXVII, 21 (October 22, 1963), pp. 41, 46.
5. Pfeffer, *op. cit.*, p. 66.
6. Healey, *op. cit.*, p. 126.
7. Ernst Troeltsch, *The Social Teaching of the Christian Churches*, 2 vols. (New York: Harper Torchbooks, 1960).
8. Conrad Henry Moehlman, *School and Church* (New York: Harper, 1944), p. ix.
9. Abington v. Schempp and Murray v. Curlett (June 17, 1963), Part V.
10. This is the suggestion of Robert W. Lynn, "Religion in the Public Schools," *Christianity and Crisis*, XXII, 13 (July 23, 1962), pp. 130–131.

11

The French and German Traditions

The traditional European way of organizing religious instruction has been to give state support to an established church and to delegate educational responsibility to it. Under the monarchy, a union of throne and altar was a solution for many otherwise difficult problems. Today, religious instruction continues to be part of the normal education for citizenship in most West European countries. It is not limited to privately supported parochial institutions or Sunday Schools, but is part of the program of the state schools. In the United States, Anabaptist frontier piety joined Enlightenment conviction in making religion a personal if not a private matter. A variety of denominations, no one of which can claim full dominance, live together in the same land. Protestant sectarian groups such as the Methodists and Baptists have supported a non-confessional state school in both England and the United States. By contrast, the Lutherans and Anglicans have taken a larger interest in parochial education, reflecting the experience of community responsibility in Germany and England respectively. However, the principle of organization has not been one of establishment but voluntarism. Membership in the religious community is not by birth, as in the case of national citizenship. Of course, family traditions are generally determinative. Still, the citizen can change denominations or religion, even withdraw from all religious activities, without political discrimination.

The American public school grew with the nation, serving a positive purpose of social integration. The state-supported educational system expanded with economic and geographical development and by and large has been untrammelled by religious disputes. Yet the public school has not been intentionally irreligious. Atheism has not belonged to the American dream.[1] Rush Welter argues that the American belief in equalitarianism in public education was more an expression of democratic idealism than of republicanism.[2] It came into its own politically with the Jacksonian revolution. Since the early part of the last century, the ideal of free universal education has been supported by both conservatives and liberals alike. School policy in the United States has been almost the exact reverse of the French or Russian systems of centralization. The public school has been a popular and lay institution under local control. Although reflecting the general democratic commitment of the national ethos, it has not been predominantly political in orientation. By and large, it has been free from interference in the change of national administrations. All major political parties have agreed on its worth and provided funds for its implementation.

There seems little immediate possibility of a school policy dominated by religion, any more than of overt persecution of the churches. American pluralism offers an atmosphere nominally favorable to religion. There are other dangers: uniquely religious functions and ideals are compromised. "Piety along the Potomac" has at times threatened to make religion an ideological sanction for the status quo rather than a vehicle for criticism. Official recognition of religion in public utterances too often does not make sufficiently clear that the Church and not the state is the primary community of redemption. American politics has been spared clerical-lay antagonisms which have accompanied the development of religiously oriented political parties in Europe. Growth of such parties does not seem imminent, much less desirable. Yet the relationship of religion to free public education has not been solved in any positive way. In the Middle Ages, the Church had responsibility for many services now cared for by the state. It was the principal educational agency, essentially international in character. Following the Reformation, school organization was increasingly national in character. In the United States, the variety of Protestant groups was such that no religious party alone could successfully accomplish the education of the entire citizenry.

It is informative to compare the history of public education in France with that in the United States, although great care must be taken in drawing any possible parallels. Madison was critical of the way in which private societies came between the French people and their government.[3] He championed disestablishment in the United States more on political than on religious grounds. The French Revolution was more explicitly anticlerical than the earlier North American struggle for freedom from colonialism.[4] Following the extremes of Jacobin rule, Napoleon re-established the Roman Catholic Church in an attempt to restore national unity as well as to secure support for his regime. Although jurisdiction over the French clergy was returned to the papacy, education was reserved to the state and centralized in a single system. More than ever in the United States, an attempt was made to unify it ideologically as well as institutionally. Traditions of centralized control, continuing to the present, limit individual initiative. For the

Church, the values of cooperation with Napoleon out-
weighed the disadvantages, especially after the persecution
of the Revolution. It was clear enough that the Emperor
wished to use re-establishment for his own political ends,
even as he had directed the emancipation of the Jews to
French national interests. His contempt for religious authority was clear in the demands he made on the Pope while
holding the head of the Church prisoner. In the end, the
Church's prestige was enhanced as the spiritual ruler resisted
heroically.

Following Napoleon's defeat, the Roman Catholic cause
was identified with monarchy throughout Europe. In
France, its educational privileges were challenged by growing republican sentiment during the nineteenth century.
Following the establishment of the Third Republic, the
public schools were made a non-religious lay institution.
The teaching orders were suppressed. Anticlericalism became vocal in the claim that Church influence in education
meant loyalty to the old regime. Early in the twentieth
century, church and state were officially separated. In the
end, the Pope encouraged French Roman Catholics to accept republicanism as the wish of the majority of the nation.
However, he was not prepared to give up the privileges of
establishment. It is of little avail today to argue whether
the earlier identification of the papacy with the cause of
popular democracy rather than monarchy in the spirit of
Lamennais, would have changed subsequent history. Un-
fortunately, neither church nor state were ready for such a
development in the first half of the nineteenth century. The
tensions of French religious life have their roots not only
in the Revolution but in the earlier decadence of the establishment in the eighteenth century. Subservient to the state,
the religious community was unable to combat the growing
rationalism and skepticism effectively. The conflict between

ecclesiastical and secular ideals has left a schism in French life which continues to the present.

One cannot easily compare the European with the North American situation; there were fundamentally different needs and problems. The United States was a newly independent, strongly self-conscious nation. As Max Lerner has pointed out, the American republic had the good fortune of expansion across the continent in an era of new invention as well as industrialization. Free public education as well as popular piety contributed to a growing democratic consensus. National unification came only at the price of a bloody struggle over slavery which was won not by idealism alone, but by Northern industrial might. In spite of the rise of the "robber barons," there was no class consciousness comparable to that in Europe. Even with establishment, a very opposite development took place in Europe than in North America, namely, dechristianization. It had one of its most disastrous results in the loss of the working classes from the Church, which, as a later Pope remarked, was the tragedy of the century.[5] Dansette, a sympathetic interpreter of Roman Catholic interests, has pointed out the general isolation of ecclesiastical leadership from the masses. Leo XIII's famous encyclical *Rerum Novarum* came late in the century. By and large, organized religion on the continent did not supply a program for the working classes who lived increasingly in an urbanized, secularized world.

French Roman Catholicism has found a vital place in national life only by reorienting itself socially. To be sure, it did recapture the loyalties of the conservative middle class which was shocked by radical rule in Paris following the Franco-Prussian War. Often under financial stress and in the face of overt repression, Roman Catholics did manage to maintain their own free schools. Today, an appreciable number of pupils at the secondary level attend paro-

chial institutions. Following long struggle, major government support was granted to such schools by the decree of
April 4, 1960. Religious instruction is allowed in institutions sponsored by the state.[6] Critics of the new policy point
out that the official support of religion began in the Pétain
era. Yet it is only fair to add that the Vichy regime simply
made official a kind of cooperation which had already begun
under earlier governments. Of more basic importance is
the fact that increased acceptance of religion in education
continued in spite of reaction against the policies of the
Pétain regime. Charges of clericalism and laicism have
seemed less relevant following the suffering of two world
wars.[7] Moreover, in the struggle against the Nazis as well
as in post-war political activities, it has often been the
Roman Catholics and Communists who have been most
concerned and active. The latter have now taken up the
cry against religion in education. It is clear that Roman
Catholic leadership has not been subservient to the state, for
example, in its statements on the Algerian war. This tragic
struggle made clear the continuing lack of community moral
consensus.

By comparison with France, the struggle over the place
of religion in education in the United States has not been
marked by major anticlerical sentiment. Yet, as earlier in
Europe, it is argued that religious conviction must remain
a completely private matter while the state carries on public
life without its sanctions. In France, at least, the older
allegedly democratic neutralism has been dissipated. Religion is recognized as having a more active role either positively by the Roman Catholics, or negatively by the Communists. The occasions on which the Church served the
French nation multiplied during the Nazi occupation. For
example, it was easier to carry on some educational activities
under the sign of the cross than under the French national
symbol. The fundamental issue is no longer whether govern-

ment and religion can remain indifferent to each other, but how they are to be related. For the believer, religion brings the witness of conscience and moral integrity. For the radical secularist, it poses a continuing threat. Of course, the older state-church ideal was not at once disavowed by Roman Catholics. Now, however, from a new understanding of common needs and problems, French policy appears to be approaching a more dynamic, open relationship characteristic of a democratic pluralistic society.[8] It is not expected that the Church will dominate culture or serve as a state agency. On the other hand, the state should not attempt to control or regulate religion as under a totalitarian regime. Instead, religion should have a responsible public voice but not special privilege with the support of state power.

It would be a mistake to suppose that the granting of tax support for church schools has brought an end to all earlier antitheses in the body politic. The earlier church-state struggle led to the establishment of a secular, government-controlled system of public education. The larger question of the values which are to be accepted in the life of the nation remains; the struggle between Marxist and non-Marxist is not ended. The charge continues that overt political pressure for school subsidy led to identification of the Roman Catholic position with the right of center, especially in the activities of Edouard Lizop and his "Association Parlementaire pour la Liberté de l'Enseignement."[9] The background of the tension between right and extreme left is assuredly the break-up of an earlier religious common sense. Would a more flexible, less absolutist position in the past have mitigated the long clerical-laicist struggle? Of course, church-state struggles cannot be resolved by utopian judgments about education or public life in general. Yet one may ask why religion was not more free from the state in the past. Was the support of a particular confessional position by force as well as the continuing union of throne and altar really necessary? French politics has been more dogmatic, less pragmatic than its British and American counterparts.

By contrast, Germany has not had as overt an anticlericalism as France. A limited form of establishment continues even in the Federal Republic, as church tax is collected by the government.[10] Religious instruction is an ordinary subject in state schools and taught under Roman Catholic or Protestant sponsorship. Education, primarily a church function in the Middle Ages, was subjected to confessional division following the Reformation. It continued under Protestant or Roman Catholic direction, depending on the religion of the ruling prince. As schools came increasingly under state control in the modern period, religious instruction continued. Until the end of the Second World War, confessional divisions were largely geographical. The maximum demand for the exclusion of religion from state-supported schools came in the Weimar Republic. A protracted struggle ended in a compromise which allowed local provincial determination of policy. Following the Second World War, there has been a more positive recognition of the need for religious training. In some states, teachers are provided by the churches. In the majority, however, special training is given to public school teachers who wish to participate in religious instruction, under Roman Catholic or Protestant supervision. Parents can choose to have their children excluded from classes in religion; however, the subject is not taught at a special hour at the beginning or end of the day.

The weakness of the German procedure, for the American point of view, is that it does not relate instruction directly to parish life. To be sure, this is less true at the primary level where children are separated in confessional schools. Yet, too often following baptism and confirmation, contact with the local parish can be nominal. One is baptized, married and buried ecclesiastically. In the United States, religious instruction is generally related more directly to the active participation of the family. On the other hand, attention is not limited to a single day per week as in American Sunday Schools. In general, teaching is better than when conducted by a voluntarily recruited lay staff. With state support, there are adequate funds for the instruction of staff as well as the development of a thoughtful pedagogical approach. Furthermore, the pupil is enabled to relate what he learns to his other subjects. Religion is understood to be a necessary and legitimate part of the school program.

Recent German experience, in a different way from that of French Roman Catholics, has made clear the necessity of freedom for the Church. German Protestants still hold to the idea of a general "Landeskirche" for an area, as against the denominational forms of organization in the United States. Yet they are more clear than before that the church must be separated from the state. The subordination of religion to the regime reached its climax under the Nazis, as the party attempted to impose "German Christianity," in fact antisemitism, through school religious instruction.[11] To the members of the Confessing Church who resisted, the essential truth of Christianity was threatened. The issue was not simply one of freedom of conscience. The Church could not be faithful to itself without protest. The matter became urgent with respect to the communication of Christian faith to the new generation. Roman Catholicism, although not a German state organization as the Protestant "Landeskirchen," faced a similar problem. Early in the Nazi period, the Vatican signed a concordat with the German government, expecting independence for its educational work and an end to the struggle over the "school question." Shortly thereafter, Nazi interference in Roman Catholic Church affairs became explicit and growing.[12]

In fact, the struggle of the Church against state control antedates modern totalitarianism by long centuries. For

Christians, there is a necessary and inevitable church-state tension. It arises from the fact that the Christian community is not identical simply with the political group, much less with folk or race; it claims a more universal loyalty. The often expressed hope that church-state tension can be resolved by government indifference to the claims of religion now appears to be utopian. There are requirements in the area of morality and practice which are not to be compromised in any political consensus. Such issues of principle cannot be ignored in any general teaching about religion. Not only do the high religions limit the absolutism of the state. They have important institutional bases, ritual and teaching authority, which ought not to be under state control. The problem of religious education, viewed from the perspective of the Christian Church, is one of making the claims of God effective among men for their salvation. Synthesis with culture is secondary. No doubt, the perennial tension between the religious community and the world about it is viewed differently in Roman Catholicism, Protestantism and Judaism. Yet all three increasingly insist that the religious society is different from the political order; the state must respect the rights of the home and church. The issue is not simply one of good will on either side, but of social structures which conform to the principles of justice.

German Protestants are now sharply critical of earlier attempts to build a Christian society. Religion too easily becomes an ideology in support of the status quo. Under state sponsorship, piety has often served a host of dubious strategies rather than bringing a realistic view of personal evil and social justice. Nineteenth-century apologetics was too much a mixture of half-truths and falsehood. Christianity is more than the best politics or science of the time. In short, a general concern about religion—as distinguished from Christian faith—was too readily a concealed secularism.

Revelation and grace are the basis of Church life. Leading Protestant spokesmen in the area of education are emphatic that it is not the task of religion to limit research or to confine knowledge.[13] Christianity should make one open for the truth without qualification in every area. Its essential principle is one of criticism, especially as it is understood in its eschatological dimensions: the kingdom of God is set in judgment against the kingdom of this world.

Roman Catholic policy in Germany has continued to attempt to build its own institutional structures.[14] Educational theory does not emphasize the antithesis between nature and grace as much as in Protestantism; instead, it seeks a synthesis between the two. The confessional school provides a context for instruction in the spirit of Catholicism as well as for worship. In Bavaria it has remained dominant and throughout much of Germany is accepted at the elementary level. Roman Catholics are explicit in affirming that their educational outlook carries an intrinsic intellectualism. However, there is less concern for "educational ideals" than before in recognition that this is an Enlightenment approach; there is more concern about practices and structures in a way of life. Truth in its immediate dimension is recognized as historical and personal, but not exclusively so; it is universal as well. Roman Catholic educational theory joins Biblical, patristic and scholastic ideas in the claim that man is a creature made in the image of God. The intellectual life has its ultimate basis in the deity, and morality is defined from obligation to him. Practically, Roman Catholic education seeks to bring all knowledge and conduct under the unity of the Absolute. It is believed that religious faith integrates culture in a way in which a simply secular context cannot. A confessional context gives a basis for an authentic intellectualism more than any simply immanentistic humanism or naturalism.

NOTES

1. Cf. Peter F. Drucker, "Organized Religion and the American Creed," *The Review of Politics*, XVIII (July 1956), pp. 296–304.

2. Welter, *op. cit.*

3. William Bosworth, *Catholicism and Crisis in Modern France* (Princeton: Princeton University Press, 1962), p. 4.

4. E. E. Y. Hales, *The Catholic Church in the Modern World* (Garden City, N.Y.: Doubleday Image, 1958).

5. Adrien Dansette, *Destin du Catholicisme Français* (Paris: Flammarion, 1957), pp. 11ff.

6. Alex Freiherr von Campenhausen, *Staat und Kirche in Frankreich* (Göttingen: Schwartz, 1962), p. 125.

7. Ulich, *op. cit.*, p. 163.

8. Von Campenhausen, *op. cit.*, p. 157.

9. Bosworth, *op. cit.*, pp. 297–301.

10. Reinhard Schmoeckel, *Der Religionsunterricht* (Hermann Luchterhand Verlag, 1964).

11. Heinrich Hermelink, *Kirche im Kampf* (Tübingen: Leins, 1950).

12. Hales, *op. cit.*

13. Oskar Hammelsbeck, *Volkschule in evangelischer Verantwortung* (Bochum: Kamp, 1961).

14. K. Erlinghagen, *Vom Bildungsideal zur Lebensordnung* (Freiburg: Herder, 1960).

12

The Parochial School
and Religion in Higher Education

The Roman Catholic population in the United States was very small at the time of the Revolutionary War. Even though it grew in size through immigration during the nineteenth century, it continued to be a minority with limited cultural influence.[1] When public sentiment was inflamed, Roman Catholics were sometimes set on by violence; more often, they were discriminated against socially or politically. Yet in time the national tradition of tolerance prevailed. Roman Catholics have full equality with other citizens. To be sure, there are lingering suspicions that a Roman Catholic majority might change governmental structures. Most responsible commentators, however, agree that the Roman Catholic hierarchy has come to recognize the values inherent in the separation of church and state in the United States.[2] Its profession that it does not seek to replace the prevailing pluralism by any form of establishment is made in good faith. No doubt, its pastoral consciousness extends into education. Moreover, the Roman Catholic Church in the United States cannot regard itself simply as one party among others;

on its view, it is the one true Church of Christ. Papal
encyclicals consider state support for parochial schools as a
matter of distributive justice.[3] Confessional tensions have
come to center on this issue in particular. Roman Catholics
continue to bear the memory of a defensive past. Other
parties in the community feel threatened by the growth of
parochial school enrollments, even though Roman Catholics
number less than a quarter of the population.

It would be a mistake to suppose that the American environment is any longer hostile to Roman Catholicism. Old
barriers have been destroyed. New voices of Protestant cooperation are to be heard by any who wish to listen. The
first major conference on church-state relations sponsored
by the National Council of the Churches of Christ (Columbus, Ohio, February 4–7, 1964) encouraged Roman Catholic
observers because it refused to take a simply separationist
position.[4] It voted against a complete ban on aid to parochial
education, although it did not advocate a general subsidy.
Msgr. George G. Higgins, Director of the National Catholic
Welfare Conference's Social Action Department, was so encouraged by the conference as to propose a joint meeting
of Roman Catholics and Protestants to discuss church-state
issues. *Interchurch News* quoted him as saying: "there
will be possible in the future a closer relationship and dialogue among Catholics and Protestants." [5]

The relation of Roman Catholic parochial schools to the
problems of education in general is a double one. What if
any support should such schools receive from public funds?
This question is a general public concern, debated by all
citizens. Irrespective of how the constitutionality of such
grants is adjudged by the courts, parochial schools will continually re-evaluate their own policies in view of existing
problems. Such re-evaluation, now under way more inten-
sively than before, is primarily a matter for Roman Catholics
themselves. After all, it is they who attend and support their

own parochial institutions. Yet, as James O'Gara has pointed out, it is not possible to separate the Catholic school fully from the larger issues of culture.[6]

Mary Perkins Ryan, a Roman Catholic mother of five boys who have attended both parochial and public schools, has recently written, *Are Parochial Schools the Answer?*[7] She joins discerning judgment of the problems of both types of institutions with concern to implement the work of the Second Vatican Council. In particular, she criticizes Roman Catholic lay persons who do not take seriously the papal social concern for the whole of society. Too often, they are satisfied that their child is safe in a parochial school and leave all leadership to the clergy and members of the religious orders. They are not sensitive to the need for renewal of the laity, to which the Council has given special attention. Mrs. Ryan also protests against a lingering defensive mentality among her fellow Catholics: the siege is now over! American society is not anti-Catholic, she reports. Rejecting such a negative attitude, Roman Catholics should not concentrate all their resources on a system of parish education which is less necessary to an independent life in the United States than in earlier decades. Parish and other religious work should receive attention as major areas of renewal. As the Bishop of Manchester, New Hampshire, has indicated in his Foreword to Mrs. Ryan's book, her view, to say the least, is debatable. It is not accepted by a large number of the staff members who are making personal sacrifices for the maintenance of parochial schools. Yet this much is clear: there are new problems in changed circumstances. The Roman Catholic approach to questions of education may be expected to be a many-sided one. Roman Catholics have a legitimate and necessary concern for the place of religion in public education.

The American hierarchy issued the following statement in 1955: "The rise and vigorous expansion of the American educational system is cited, correctly, as one of the major achievements of Western civilization. . . . It would be blind prejudice which would refuse to acknowledge, in this connection, the tremendous accomplishment of public educational agencies." [8] A recent paper issued by the committee of Catholic diocesan school superintendents reads: "If the reminder is needed for the few—the public school is here to stay. The choices then are simple. . . . The alternatives are either to support and strengthen a form of public education which, of necessity, will take place within a less than perfect atmosphere, or to continue to promote by our indifference the purely secular school which we can then continue to condemn for its godlessness." [9] Father Neil G. McCluskey, one of the most knowledgable students of parochial school problems in the United States, writes: "Today, Catholics are coming to see, by and large, that the old ideal of every Catholic child in a Catholic school is impossibly utopian. Today, non-Catholics are gradually conceding—again, by and large—that the religious school is here to stay and that it is a significant part of American education (whether desirable or not) ." [10]

At present, approximately 14% of the school population is in parochial schools.[11] During the past two decades, public school enrollments increased 36%, non-public school enrollments, 118%. Roman Catholic education is conducted in a particular context of faith and devotion. The Church's position is stated officially in Pope Pius XI's encyclical, "On the Education of Youth." [12] It treats of three different societies. The first society, the family, has a special right to determine the education of children. It is not, however, self-complete as is the second society, the state, which has responsibility for the this-worldly destiny of its citizens. Finally, the Church, a third society, perfect and supernatural, directs man to his eternal destiny. These different orders are not necessarily in conflict, but should sustain each other in their mutual responsibilities. For example, the Church does not destroy but strengthens the family and the state. As a visible society, it has authority and responsibility to educate. Its role is one of intellectual guidance as well as moral encouragement. Non-Catholics should be careful not to mistake the consistency or the integrity of the Roman Catholic position as it is based on papal encyclicals. It is that common secular instruction is not regarded as enough. Most desirable is a total Catholic milieu for education and growth. Teaching is not simply information or experiment; it involves the communication of a common tradition at the levels of *both* thought *and* practice.

It is not meaningless to point out that separation of church and state has contributed in its own way to the American Roman Catholic achievement. Parochial schools were established in part as a defense against Protestant as well as secular influence. Yet they have been successful in part because of the national ethos. Anticlericalism has been at a minimum. The clergy were not identified with the old status quo of the monarchy as in continental Europe. Father John Courtney Murray, among others, has attempted to reinterpret papal encyclicals in view of the unique development of life and thought in the United States.[13] Such re-evaluation recognizes that disestablishment has brought new freedom and vitality. Roman Catholic growth has been phenomenal, from a church of immigrants to the largest religious body in the nation. The Roman Catholic parochial school system is the most extensive of any in the world, developed without state funds. In fact, American Roman Catholics have been more faithful in participation and less nationalistic than their co-religionists in many other lands.

Neil G. McCluskey finds a changing pattern emerging to meet new conditions: "Catholic leadership in the United States is not doing an about-face, but is facing up to some of the hard realities of the present and inviting challenges of the future." [14] McCluskey reports that four major problems have been inherited from the past: 1. clerical domination of the schools; 2. over-commitment to the elementary school; 3. confusion of the academic mandate and the pastoral charge; 4. substitution of the school for the family and the Church as the primary agent in the religious formation of the child. McCluskey—who has worked hard and long in support of parochial education—shares with other clergy a concern for its effect on parish life in general. He surmises that probably 75 percent of the time and energy of the pastor and his assistant is spent in fund-raising for the parish school. Imagination and initiative are sapped. There is too little time and energy left over to train parents or to build an effective religious education program for the hundreds of Roman Catholic children in the public schools. Positively, Father McCluskey notes that academic standards have been raised significantly since the organization of the National Sister Formation Conference in 1951; the period of teacher preparation and study has been extended. It is also important to note that the proportion of lay teachers in Roman Catholic elementary schools has increased sharply from 7.1% in 1950 to 33.2% in 1963.

The Roman Catholic ideal is a universal one, not determined primarily from American needs or problems. How are its principles to be applied to existing practice? There is a growing body of evaluation and criticism whose realism bespeaks hope for the future. John F. Mahoney, Associate Professor of English at the University of Detroit, has written discerningly of the "Paradoxes of Parochial Schools." [15] Beginning at the most practical level, he calls attention to the lack of staff and buildings which has led to overcrowding as well as double sessions in many Roman Catholic institutions. Accredited personnel are often in short supply, he reports. Before the Second World War parochial schools compared rather well with public educational institutions. Problems and difficulties have increased in the competition of the post-war era. Professor Mahoney believes that Roman Catholics should continue to fight for legislation in support of the welfare benefits allowed by the courts, for example, bus transportation. Yet he warns most particularly that this struggle should not blind them to larger problems. Whatever the outcome of the attempt to secure government support, the ideal of academic excellence must not be abandoned.

Father McCluskey believes that more attention must be given to other levels than the elementary school.[16] The Third Plenary Council of Baltimore in 1884 envisaged that an elementary school would be established near every Church "within two years." Of course, this level of education remains important in the formation of character. Now a much larger part of the population than before attend high school and college. Father McCluskey points out that the most lasting loyalties attach psychologically to these institutions. Permanent relationships are formed in extracurricular activities as well as course studies. No doubt, the cost of more advanced instruction is larger than in the elementary school. Professor Mahoney points out that there is continuing pressure to compromise basic issues of principle in the face of present needs.[17] Roman Catholic institutions do not have parallel structures comparable with their secular counterparts at all levels. Not only are there scientific and technical pressures. There is the demand that graduates shall be able to compete successfully in various areas of business and professional life.

Can Roman Catholic education be faithful to its own specific traditions and yet take on more contemporary relevance? Mahoney protests that in the attempt to meet educational standards, Roman Catholic institutions have tended to copy secular schools. Even religious teaching at times has been set in a social science context.[18] Mahoney urges that Roman Catholics must involve themselves in public as well as private education lest they lose leadership in both areas and be left with only a lagging parochial school system. This proposal may seem a drastic one in view of the present needs of church-sponsored institutions. Yet it reflects continuing concern among Roman Catholic leaders that their Church look beyond its own parochial institutions. If Roman Catholicism is to have a hearing outside of its own educational circles, it may be added, it must do so in terms of ideas more than of institutional strength. Assuredly, limited educational contexts can support the development of full positive insights in a particular tradition. Nonetheless, dialogue with other points of view, scientific as well as political and social, and participation in community life, are prerequisite to a significant hearing in the modern world. Daniel Callahan, Associate Editor of *Commonweal*, in a discerning study describes the new role which Roman Catholic leadership envisages for the layman.[19] He makes doubly clear that the defensive orientation present in some aspects of American Roman Catholic life is no longer acceptable.

Karl Rahner has pointed out that the non-religious areas of existence in contrast to former times have become areas of tremendous density, fullness, complication and capacity for absorption.[20] Religiously interested persons must be careful not to confuse the growth of secular understanding with secularism. Modern schools as expressions of contemporary culture are inextricably bound up with areas of decision and instruments of analysis unknown even a century and a half ago—sociology, anthropology, depth psychology, biochemistry, economic geography, technology, cybernetics, economic management and political science. A new theology of the temporal order is needed. The Christian must have more than a "booby-trap view" of the universe as only a place through which one passes to win salvation.

The Roman Catholic parochial school was not a major force in the United States at the time of the writing of the Constitution. Community structures of education have been changed with its expansion in recent decades, especially in the larger Eastern cities. Callahan has called the problem of state support a briar patch. Explicit legislation granting such support would be politically controversial long before it reached the courts. Callahan is correct in arguing that it is surrounded by a tangle of social, cultural, historical and educational considerations. However, such a distinguished legal authority as Professor Wilbur G. Katz of the University of Wisconsin, and formerly Dean of the Law School at the University of Chicago, argues that the courts have not ruled against aid to parochial schools in support of general education. A major problem, even if such aid were accepted by the courts, would be the wide diversity of religious denominations in the United States. Whereas the Roman Catholic Church has a well developed system of parochial schools, most Protestant bodies do not. A grant of state funds would assuredly evoke a variety of second-rate Protestant institutions which, after the first initial wave of enthusiasm, would bring little gain for religion or education. The danger which Msgr. D'Amour has foreseen with respect to shared-time programs would become more acute: once the doors were open, new educational sponsorship could arise from almost everywhere to the detriment of existing educational facilities. There is the further question as to whether such subsidy would not be regarded by the courts as multiple establishment, an arrangement which they have already opposed.

Roman Catholic leadership is aware of the possibility, indeed the probability, that no major direct grants will be made to parochial schools in the near future. It is at this point that ecumenical concern becomes increasingly important, not only in winning a wider hearing for religious education, but in positive interfaith policies throughout education in general. If the Supreme Court would regard direct aid to religious education as a form of establishment, as seems probable, should not religious forces explore other strategies, such as shared time and teaching about religion? Full securalism is not yet accomplished, but it is potential! Much will depend on the attitudes of religiously committed persons as well as on strategies used by their leaders to defend openness toward religion. We believe that the major problem is one of educational policy, the free exercise of religion, and not the separation of church and state. Questions of financial cost, as in the McCollum and Regents' Prayer cases, do not go to the heart of the issue. How can religion be recognized in education without violating the conscience of the uncommitted or usurping the prerogatives of the religious community?

First consideration must be given to matters of education and public welfare, not to partisan pleading. Resourcefulness and flexibility, tolerance as well as the refusal of oversimplified answers are needed on all sides. The initiative of religious agencies is recognized as legitimate and indeed necessary; it ought not to be circumscribed. The danger, however, is that in the face of rebuffs, religious education will develop toward greater defensiveness rather than a more open attempt to meet modern needs and issues. The latter is indispensable if religious institutions are to have significant influence on education in general.

Recent Congressional enactment has authorized expenditure of federal funds in support of expansion of facilities in higher education, whether or not such education is under simply private, church or state sponsorship.[21] To be sure, the projects envisaged are not those of religious education! Yet a more generous policy toward church-sponsored education than at the elementary and high school levels, has been enacted in the new legislation. Its special purpose is to help meet the costs of rapid expansion at the college and university level. Even with such legislation, an ever-increasing percentage of the school population will be enrolled in state universities. The diversity of American educational life is encouraged by the new legislation; all higher education need not be of the same type. Such support for a variety of kinds of schools was not brought about primarily by ecclesiastical pressure. Instead, there was a larger consensus in the American community about what should be done at the higher rather than at the lower levels. There seems a good possibility that the precedents established will be accepted by the courts.

No doubt, there will be protests that any college or university with effective denominational discipline should not receive government subsidy. The obvious effect of such a position, if adopted, would be to restrict the role of religion in higher education, altering long-standing traditions. Colleges and universities have been characterized by a greater diversity of sponsorship than in the elementary or high schools. Church-related institutions vary widely. Some have intensive programs of worship and study; others are only nominally religious. State university practice is not uniform. A number of state schools have departments of religion; a few institutions have even sponsored chapel programs. The proposal to refuse all federal aid to any program of higher education which includes religion has a double limitation: it fails to consider that students can be exposed more easily to a variety of positions, as they are more mature. Religious ideas can be considered from all points of view, whether under state or denominational auspices. Secondly, many of the services rendered by denominational schools are non-religious. Are these institutions to be penalized for their religious loyalties? The proposal comes at a time when virtually all colleges and universities are increasingly dependent on government subsidy for a variety of types of support, including research grants.

The majority of responsible university officials probably would regard an unqualified secularization as leading to the impoverishment of education and restricting the scope of inquiry into the basic problems of education. It would not encourage the free exercise of religion, but rather its restriction. How can there be freedom without knowledge of different points of view? Why should not Judaism and Christianity as well as other world religions have a fair hearing in the classroom? Secularism has been most vocal in institutions of higher learning. It deserves to have its case heard openly pro and con, but not to be established as the only "religious position"! A ban against theology precludes fair consideration of the contrary arguments; knowledge is restricted in what is in fact a denial of the American tradition of pluralism. Paradoxically, colleges and universities have succeeded, more than ever before, in teaching religion on an objective, non-sectarian basis.[22] Any attempt to limit such teaching would be especially unfortunate in view of the fact that interfaith communication has been most possible at the level of colleges and universities. Our society must continually reappraise its values and beliefs in view of the continuing struggle against totalitarianism. If religion is vital to democracy, neither its study nor devotion should be driven underground.

Since the beginning of our country, the majority of its colleges and universities have been careful not to exclude religion. Jefferson made it part of the curriculum in a limited form at the University of Virginia, urging that facts should predominate over emotion in its studies.[23] Is it not in his spirit to recognize all major traditions, Roman Catholic, Protestant and Jewish? Faculty members should have freedom to speak for each of them. Differences ought not to be ignored in alleged neutrality. Education cannot be simply silent, especially at the college and university level. Like other public institutions, both elementary and high schools, universities teach about religion in history, literature and art as well as philosophy. The educational question concerns the mode of its interpretation; is teaching to be responsible and informed? Legitimate concern for and teaching about religion in the state universities needs to be supplemented from schools belonging to particular traditions. Higher education is enriched by the presence of a Jewish University such as Brandeis, Roman Catholic schools such as Fordham and Notre Dame as well as by clearly identified Protestant institutions. The notion that scholarship in these schools is simply partisan is mistaken. On the contrary, it is enriched by its particular loyalties. No one form of academic organization should receive exclusive government support in a pluralistic society, although state universities will receive the major grants of funds for instruction. In fact, public control does not necessarily assure any more freedom than church sponsorship. It is diversity and not uniformity which belongs to democracy.

NOTES

1. Stokes and Pfeffer, *op. cit.*, p. 238.
2. Herberg, *op. cit.*
3. *Rappresentanti in terra* (December 31, 1929), Christian Education of Youth. Anne Freemantle, *The Papal Encyclicals in Their Historical Context* (New York: Mentor, 1963), pp. 224–227.
4. *Interchurch News,* Vol. V, No. 7 (March 1964), p. 1.
5. *Ibid.*
6. *Commonweal,* Vol. 79, No. 18 (January 31, 1964). All of the following articles cited from *Commonweal* are from this special issue on religion and education.
7. Mary Perkins Ryan, *Are Parochial Schools the Answer?* (New York: Holt, Rinehart and Winston, 1964).
8. Karl Rahner, *Sendung und Gnade* (Innsbruck: Tyrolia, 1959), pp. 13–47,

is an exposition of his important idea of "diaspora." The first two volumes of this work have already been published in English by Sheed and Ward: *The Christian Commitment* (1963) and *Theology for Renewal* (1964). A third volume is scheduled for publication in 1966.

9. *Ibid.,* p. 537.
10. McCluskey, "A Changing Pattern," *Commonweal, op. cit.,* p. 507.
11. *Ibid.*
12. Freemantle, *op. cit.*
13. John Courtney Murray, *We Hold These Truths* (New York: Sheed and Ward, 1960).
14. McCluskey, "A Changing Pattern," *Commonweal op. cit.,* pp. 507ff.
15. *Catholic World* (April 1964), pp. 28–33.
16. McCluskey, *Commonweal.*
17. Mahoney, *op. cit.*
18. *Ibid.*
19. Daniel Callahan, *The Mind of the Catholic Layman* (New York: Scribner, 1963).
20. *Commonweal, op. cit.,* pp. 533ff.
21. College Academic Facilities Act, signed by the President, December 16, 1963.
22. Drinan, *op. cit.,* pp. 179–181. Blanshard, *op. cit.,* pp. 145–150.
23. Healey, *op. cit.,* pp. 216–218.

13

Teaching About Religion

The Supreme Court decision is positive in this respect at least: It encourages responsible teaching about religion.

It might well be said that one's education is not complete without a study of comparative religion or the history of religion and its relationship to the advancement of civilization. It certainly may be said that the Bible is worthy of study for its literary and historic qualities. Nothing we have said here indicates that such study of the Bible or religion, when presented objectively as part of a secular program of education, may not be effected consistent with the First Amendment.[1]

The question remains, whether institutional leadership is prepared to recognize and support such teaching. Is it willing to understand the role of religion in public education as more than denominational apologetics or propagation of particular confessional points of view? If the alternative is only between one type of doctrine or another, Roman Catholic, Protestant or Jewish, such teaching is clearly illegal in the public school. But the Supreme Court has ruled that it is possible to teach about religion. Religion, we have argued, is

153

both many-sided and rich in meaning. Religious ideas deserve a fair hearing—Roman Catholic and Jewish as well as
Protestant. The non-Western religions should not be ignored,
although our culture is not as indebted to them as to the
Hebrew-Christian tradition. It is crucial to the whole problem of religion in education that it be understood in its
widest meaning. Not just particular sectarian claims, but an
entire world view is in question.

It is our thesis that specific information about religion
has a legitimate place in the public school curriculum.
Teaching forms a positive or negative intellectual image of
religion. If the school assumes a disinterested or secularist
outlook, the child is conditioned accordingly. Throughout
most of history, from the primitive to the present world
conflict, religious issues have been at stake. Any curriculum
which seeks to avoid them is partisan to the extreme. The
fall of Rome, the building of the cathedrals, the Crusades,
the Reformation and the rise of low church traditions on
the frontier in the United States all belong to our common
history. Modern problems of war, racial discrimination and
family life have, in the end, religious implications. No more
are they to be ignored because they invite controversy than
can religion be relegated to irrelevance. It is impossible to
understand the basic traditions of American life apart from
a knowledge of the Bible and Christian history. This is clear,
for example, in the frequent references to the Bible in the
pronouncements of Abraham Lincoln. Lincoln did not use
the Bible as a sectarian book, but as a rich source of life
meanings. Not to include material in the curriculum about
Judaism and Christianity is equally as biased as to limit
teaching to a particular partisan meaning.

Religious parents have the right to expect that their faith
should not be represented negatively, but be presented in
its full positive efficacy. We have already considered the
study by a special committee of the American Council of

Education.[2] Such studies indicate that a common curriculum, known and agreed upon as relevant by the major
religious leaders in the community, can make clear that
other than sectarian issues are at stake in classroom instruction about religion. To be sure, consensus about appropriate
material requires interfaith dialogue between different
groups, Protestant, Roman Catholic and Jewish. But this,
we feel, is far more in the spirit of Jefferson than the attempt to ban all religious ideas. Each group has a particular
heritage of its own. This fact need not preclude objectivity
of teaching. A study of world religions makes clear a variety
of vital issues about the meaning of life and death; they
have concerned mankind in the past as in the present. In
an era of mass communication and closer interrelation of
nations, Hinduism, Buddhism and Islam are increasingly
related to the events of American life. Their adherents and
their conviction are ever more a part of our world. Recognition of religious diversity can be a means of enrichment
as well as self-understanding as the student matures.

Father John Courtney Murray has emphasized that there
are three basic positions to be considered in Western religion, Roman Catholic, Protestant and Jewish.[3] These should
not be taught about as if they were a single platform! Teaching about religion in general is particularly dubious. Father Murray believes that particular epistemologies as well
as facts about conflicting positions—clearly identifying differences—can have a legitimate place in general discussion.
With these considerations in view, one can say that ideally
instruction about religion should be carried on at a minimum of three different levels. First, theory of knowledge
needs to make clear the legitimacy of religious expression—
symbolism, sacrament and story. A simply naturalistic or
positivistic interpretation of religion is inadequate. Catholicism rightly emphasizes that man's natural religious quest
is fulfilled by grace. Religious feelings are not prompted

simply by fear, economic and social causes, sex, etc., but by man's need for God. Mankind has deeper religious sensitivity than pragmatism or scientism have ever allowed. It is most important to distinguish between primitive and high religions, superstition and faith. Sacramentalism is not magic or religious authority necessarily arbitrary.

Secondly, religious insight ought to be related to the concerns of the larger philosophical tradition. Here, again, history and the study of particular traditions should have primacy over generalization. The history of philosophy poses questions which cannot be given just an empirical or pragmatic answer! They are cosmological as well as personal. Christian theology developed in conscious relation to Western philosophy. Augustine and Aquinas, for example, did not separate faith and reason completely. Reason was to be accepted as a God-given gift and followed as far as possible; in the end, it cannot replace revelation. Perhaps the greatest immediate service organized religion could do for education would be to insist on the study of the *philosophia perennis* at every level of teaching. Without doubt, a considerable part of contemporary philosophical reflection has been limited to theory of knowledge or even word analysis; it has not been interested in religious questions. However, there is also renewed concern for theology in the understanding that it cannot be replaced by philosophy. An understanding of the problems of the *philosophia perennis* makes for integrity of teaching. Religious questions become intellectually meaningful and not just issues of pious sentiment or "faith alone." Although specific courses in the history of philosophy are most appropriate at the advanced levels of instruction, its problems are relevant throughout the curriculum.

Thirdly, teaching about religion should include facts about particular positions. The world faiths have structures, recurrent themes of affirmation which can be studied historically.[4] Religious knowledge is not just subjective, but belongs to a particular community. To put the matter bluntly, no major religion allows that one man's ideas are as good as another's. It is an abuse to equate such relativism with freedom of conscience. Judaism and Christianity claim levels of insight which are grounded in reality and thus transcend the individual consciousness.[5] Granted that the historical study of facts about religion does not lead to personal faith, it can nonetheless reduce confusion. It can make clear how much Jewish and Christian ideas have determined the basic outlook of our culture and carry with them what has been so often lacking in contemporary education—an abiding sense of right and wrong. A phenomenological investigation of their content opens the possibility of discussion in education; they can speak for themselves against secularist competition. Study need not be simply apologetic, but it ought not to cover up "faith differences" by alleged objective scholarship.

Although morality or religious belief cannot be prescribed by the public schools, education does have a responsibility to make the student conscious of their highest expressions. Honesty in historical scholarship requires acknowledgment of the fact that religions have at times supported intolerance, persecution and warfare. Their leaders have imposed a variety of types of behavior which are now recognized as unethical on common sense standards. Child sacrifice, sacred prostitution and holy war all belong to the history of religion. These facts cannot be glossed over, but need to be explained in healthy realism. The student ought not to be led to believe that all forms of Western religion have been without fault, much less that all persons of non-Western conviction lack good will. Historical study serves to bring the underlying theistic affirmation about the nature and destiny of man into clearer focus. Jews, Roman Catholics and Protestants all believe that man is not the master of his own destiny. He is responsible to a higher being who alone will finally vanquish evil and establish the good. Human existence in the present space-time world is not an end in itself, but subject to the law of God.

Surely full responsibility of mature understanding ought not to be placed on small children. Nonetheless, life attitudes are formed at an early age while learning is still done by story and example. Not only are the Bible and Christian history prerequisite to understanding Western civilization; they deserve attention in themselves. In Great Britain, government schools include such material in the curriculum from a common syllabus agreed on by major religious groups.[6] Granted that such procedure is not always entirely satisfactory, ought it not to be improved upon rather than rejected in neglect of religion? More than in the past, there is a wide consensus of agreement among Protestant, Roman Catholic and Jewish scholars on historical questions. Protestant and Roman Catholic scholarship will probably produce a common translation of the Bible before the turn of the century. Of course, outstanding disagreements remain. When understood in their historical background, they can be treated with greater objectivity.

The material which can be presented in teaching about religion assuredly varies with the level of instruction. There is least difficulty in presenting a variety of points of view in college teaching; students can be exposed to a diversity of ideas without uncritical acceptance. It is interesting to note that the American Civil Liberties Union which opposed religious observance in the lower grades is prepared to regard religious activities in the colleges and universities as more than sectarian.[7] Beside emphasizing the legitimate place of religion throughout culture in general, responsible leadership should encourage development of courses specifically adapted to the subject. There are excellent precedents already at hand for such teaching both in private and public universities. Whenever possible, the teaching staff should include scholars of all three major confessions, Protestant, Roman Catholic and Jewish. Dialogue and the exchange of ideas is encouraged when a variety of points of view are represented. The outlook of instruction need not be just confessional, but historical and phenomenological. Students are stimulated when confronted by disagreement as well as agreement. Bible, Church history, religious social concern, literature as well as music, comparative religions, provide a rich variety of subject matter. Areas of agreement are much larger than is generally recognized. Dr. George Shuster of Notre Dame University has remarked:

> Mr. Justice Jackson in his day surmised that nobody could instruct in the Reformation without offending one creed or other. The fact of the matter is that this problem had long since been solved.[8]

It is most important that instruction in religion have standards of competence equal to those in other disciplines. Dean Schilling of Pennsylvania State University has pointed out that it is increasingly recognized that there is a legitimate subject matter with appropriate discipline for such teaching.[9] Responsible ecclesiastical leadership does not serve its own interests when it disregards this fact.

It is very probable that high school instruction of ten or twenty years hence will be more like the college teaching of the present. This is especially the case with respect to courses in the humanities. Why should high school teaching not include information about religion for which there is growing interest and materials at the college level? Courses should be elective with a maximum objective presentation of material. A study of Roman Catholicism, Protestantism and Judaism is especially popular in the universities. Why should the least informed elements, sectarian or secularist, block responsible teaching in the public schools? Of course, such instruction ought not to move to the high school without consultation with the major religious groups whose resources could be used to supplement class work. A Roman Catholic professor, now teaching education at the university level, was most successful in conducting a high school course on the Reformation. After he had told religious community leaders of his goals in historical study, he received fine support. Part of the reluctance to undertake such teaching lies in the difficulty of any public institution in dealing with controversy. A genuine respect for truth and learning can help to overcome partisan opposition and intolerance. However, information about religion must also win its place through responsible teaching.

Teaching about religion at the elementary and junior high school levels has its own characteristic problems. Differing points of view cannot be presented as easily as in more advanced instruction. Yet cooperation between the home, church and school can help to minimize difficulties. The issue of common prayers, however much it has attracted public attention, is not as important as a balanced educational outlook. In what context are moral values or the place of religion in culture to be appraised? Why should not teaching units in history of Judaism and Christianity be included in social studies? The churches and synagogues should be concerned to support preparation of well-written texts on such materials which convey the idea that tolerance need not be indifference! Unless certain facts about religion are presented objectively, students can hardly be expected to appreciate its contribution to the progress of humanity—a goal of instruction to which the Supreme Court has given its approval. Assuredly, teaching about religion is seldom possible without a working relationship of good will between religious and educational leadership. Teacher training is of special importance. The answer is not simply one of worship or church instruction in public school buildings. It is rather that religion should be given a fair hearing throughout the curriculum by underlining its relevance to life both in the past and the present.

It cannot be emphasized too much that instruction in the public schools about religion need not and ought not to be of a missionary character. Roman Catholic and Jewish parents have a legitimate criticism of Protestant attempts to impose an "evangelical attitude." Protestants must realize that religious subject matter cannot be limited to moral instruction alone; it needs historical content. Differences of belief must be faced openly. Many questions at issue are controversial; it is part of the integrity of education in a democracy that they should be presented objectively and fairly. We have protested against pragmatic educational theory because it so often obscures and confuses the finality of faith affirmations. We do not propose to replace it by an appeal to authority in the public schools. Instead, religious teaching should be oriented on what Roman Catholicism as well as the Enlightenment identified as natural theology. In addition, instruction should include facts about particular religions. The content is different from that of released-time teaching under denominational auspices and it is important that clear distinction be made between the two. Religious questions cannot be answered in education by custom or practical solution alone. Instead, they require sensitive evaluation which the public school cannot make fully. It must recognize that each person will struggle for personal integrity against evil as long as he lives. It cannot answer religious questions as fully as the Church, but it can help prepare students to face them meaningfully.

Let us transpose our evaluation to a Hindu, Moslem or Buddhist society. As a non-participant in these religions, Jewish or Christian parents would not want their child to join in Moslem prayers, Hindu Scripture reading or Buddhist meditation. Nor would they want a son or daughter to study a curriculum limited by the point of view of one of these religions. Besides training the child in their own religion, the parents would work for a more open cultural situation and against communalism or obscurantism. Yet it remains an open question whether one could really understand Arab history without learning about the Koran or Mohammed. Education in India would not be complete apart from knowledge of the Hindu religious tradition any more than Japanese or Chinese culture could be understood apart from Buddhism. Fair and responsible teaching about these religions, without intent of conversion, would be a legitimate educational goal. Of course, it can be argued that one should disregard religious differences for a more "scientific view" of life. Assuredly, devotees of these faiths have not always made a responsible contribution to common life; religion at times has evoked fanaticism as well as civil strife. Yet not to teach about religion would be not only to ignore a large part of history, but a major area of human need and interest. Suppose that the religiously uncommitted parent does not want his child to know anything about religions. Such a position becomes obscurantist and the curriculum truncated. In short, religion has not been a simply private matter, but a cultural force of great power—to a positive or negative degree. One ought not to suppose that it is always good or that all religions are the same. Yet significant distinction cannot be made if the subject is never discussed!

NOTES

1. Abington v. Schempp and Murray v. Curlett (June 17, 1963), Part V.
2. Chapter 4, pp. 49–54.
3. Murray, "America's Four Conspiracies," *Religion in America*, *op. cit.*
4. Mircea Eliade and Joseph M. Kitagawa, *The History of Religions: Essays in Methodology* (Chicago: University of Chicago Press, 1959).

5. Niels C. Nielsen, Jr., *The Layman Looks at World Religions* (St. Louis: Bethany, 1962).
6. Marjorie Cruickshank, *Church and State in English Education, 1870 to the Present Day* (London: Macmillan, 1963).
7. Drinan, *op. cit.,* p. 180.
8. George N. Schuster, "Religion and Education," *Commonweal, op. cit.,* p. 505.
9. *Teacher Education and Religion,* American Association of Colleges for Teacher Education (Washington, D.C., 1959).

14

The Non-Christian Religions

Can the public schools teach about the non-Christian religions of the world? Historians of culture have long recognized that the major faiths provide basic thought forms for the different civilizations in which they live. To be sure, religious belief must be considered in relation to other factors such as geography, climate and history. Yet, as Toynbee has shown, no major civilization can be understood in its development apart from a religious view of human nature and destiny.[1] As a determinant of culture, religion is more than a sectarian phenomenon. It is not simply individualistic, but more often than not carries strong social consciousness. Universal religions such as Buddhism and Christianity as well as Islam have transcended national and racial divisions. They are concerned finally and most of all with man's salvation, but even in this concern they do not neglect the present. They have expressed themselves in moral and spiritual ideals which outlive particular eras. Toynbee describes the ethically developed religions as the vehicle by which mankind advances even amid the rise and fall of empires.[2]

Christopher Dawson has commented that the study of history helps us to relativize our immediate perspectives.[3]

This is especially the case in the field of religion. Modern naturalism and individualism must be put aside for fuller understanding. A large part of mankind has lived close to intuitive and group experience. The French philosopher, Henri Bergson, made an important and necessary distinction between primitive and high religion in his book, *The Two Sources of Morality and Religion*.[4] Primitive religion, he pointed out, is defensively oriented and leads to a closed society. Group feeling is at a maximum. Both decision and responsibility are socially oriented; collective guilt is accepted. The individual is identified with the family or tribe and responds to experience by instinct and emotion rather than abstract idea. Powerful unwritten traditions and symbols control human life. The chief purpose served by primitive religion is the continuation of the group. Ceremony and ritual insure conformity with the customs believed to be necessary for fertility in the family or the protection of the tribe in time of war. Morality, in so far as it may be said to exist, is expressed in taboos which are irrational if not meaningless from a more developed point of view.

Growth away from the primitive level of life proceeds slowly. Superstition and magic all too easily perpetuate themselves. Still, the development of national religions with their more advanced cultures marks a different stage in the life of mankind. And yet, polytheistic, national religions are not necessarily moral or elevated, for change is not simply uniform or in a single direction. A decisive point was reached historically with the advent of the universal religions, most of all Buddhism and Christianity. Bergson holds that it is possible to identify the high religions by the fact that they make for an open rather than a closed society. The particularity of culture is not denied, but taken into a larger whole. Most of all, these religions teach love of fellowman; the latter is not to be destroyed as an enemy but valued as one who may attain salvation.

It is our thesis that religion is natural to man, although what is often called natural religion is not the final norm of its truth. Religious meanings belong intrinsically to human experience. They have deeper roots than fear or fantasy and cannot be dissolved into psychological or sociological factors alone. This conclusion is to be justified, most of all, from the study of the history of religion itself. Professor Mircea Eliade argues that modern research makes it possible, for the first time, to give a genuinely comprehensive and cross-cultural description of religious phenomena.[5] In short, we can now say what the religion of mankind has been in all times and places. Bernard Iddings Bell invoked a distinction from Alfred North Whitehead's Lowell Lectures, *Religion in the Making,* in explaining what religion is and does.[6] Whitehead identified four stages in the development of religion: ritual, story or myth, faith or belief, and rationalization or interpretation. Whether these are chronological or different elements in experience need not concern us here. Bell treats them as vital constituents in the religious experience and growth of each person. As such, they are of fundamental importance in teaching about religion. Protestant interpretation is likely to minimize the place of ritual, as compared with the Jewish or Roman Catholic outlook. Yet the historical importance of ritual and ceremony remains large. Attitudes and belief are expressed as often in repeated action as in creed. It is important to understand that the elements described by Whitehead can be only partially represented in teaching about religion. Ritual might be discussed, even observed, but not participated in directly by the common school.

Can teaching about world religions be more than an irrelevant, relativistic, if not naturalistic, catalogue of what different persons and societies have believed? This will depend on whether organizing principles, historical and philosophical, can be given to the curriculum. The German philosopher Karl Jaspers speaks of an axial or pivotal point in history.[7] The teaching of Confucius in China, Gotama Buddha in India, Socrates and Plato in Greece, as well as the later Hebrew prophets, all fell in a common era.[8] New traditions were initiated, often building on the religions of the past. Of course, Greek philosophy was fundamentally more speculative than Hebrew prophecy. Yet the fact remains that new outlooks and types of interpretation were established as in hardly any other single era. They were to remain dominant for subsequent centuries, continuing even into the present. Heinrich Kraemer argues that the decisive encounter between world religions—East and West—is yet to come in the future.[9] However this may be, Christian theologians are increasingly taking a more open attitude toward other faiths. This view is, indeed, the opposite of the eclecticism which too often dominates the popular mind.

It is clear that the great religions carry fundamentally different views of personal destiny as well as ultimate meaning. However, the study of the non-Christian religions ought not to be characterized by their total rejection as has too often been the case in apologetics. A knowledge of the history of religions can lead to the conviction that mankind's quest for ultimate meaning is more than a record of blind feeling. The world's great faiths, some more than others, claim to have relevance for the life of reason. Hinduism and Buddhism have been remarkable stimulants to philosophical reflection. Christianity in its own way has oriented its self-interpretation on careful, systematic reflection. The most detailed, developed metaphysic in the West grew up under Christian intellectual stimulus in the high Middle Ages, namely Thomism. Reason was valued, but not as the sole determiner or source of all meaning. Truth is believed to be grounded in a higher Reality. The religious dimension of understanding inevitably conditions philosophical experience, East and West. The history of religion by itself cannot answer the problem of truth. Yet it can show how concern for ultimate meaning has been powerful enough to remake whole societies.

Hans Küng has pointed out how important it is that the study of the history of religion should not view the classical world faiths as abstract alternatives.[10] Of course, each has its tradition and faces problems of modernization occasioned by the rise of modern science and democracy. More than this, each is today in competition with pseudo-religions or ideologies: exaggerated nationalism, scientism, communism and materialism. It is a mistake to treat the non-Christian religions simply as unbelief or idolatry, as Karl Barth has done.[11] With Judaism and Christianity, they share a deeper sense of suffering and evil as well as the hope of salvation and life after death. Their basis of insight is more profound, their analysis more searching than that of modern secular alternatives. Moreover, Küng urges that they must be regarded as a seeking after God and salvation, although on Christian premises not with full disclosure. In the study of the major world religions, it is important to avoid over-simplification of truth and untruth. Careful reading of their history can lead to a new understanding of the meaning and role of religion in human life. Their theologies cannot be simplified into mere moralism. Hinduism, Buddhism or Islam—no more than Christianity or Judaism—cannot be reduced to the Golden Rule!

Rudolph Otto pointed out how much religious meaning is concerned—most of all—with the holy.[12] For the high religions, its presence brings a sense of personal unworthiness, sin and the need for forgiveness. Man's life is set in larger dimensions in the drama of salvation. Western religion, especially, is emphatic in rejection of idolatry. God is not to be equated with his creation; he alone is worthy of complete trust and loyalty. Similarly, for Buddhism, the world of space-time is not ultimate. All symbols, even Buddha himself, are to be seen through to Nirvana. In general, the more developed religions, national or universal as distinguished from primitivive, do not regard man as just a part of nature; instead, he is understood to have unique capacities, the dignity to attain Nirvana in Hinduism or Buddhism or beatitude in Christianity.

Religion in the general Enlightment sense becomes an empty term apart from the great world faiths. It is the latter which probe questions of origin, destiny, evil, suffering, death and salvation—bringing a new dimension of understanding. Although participation in the life of a particular religion is necessary to the fullest understanding of its meaning and "mysteries," a study of its history and ideas can increase the student's knowledge of what is at stake in the claims it makes. Each of the great religions has its own special insights or kerygma; this is as much the case in Eastern as in Western religion. For example, in Buddhism, the kerygma is mediated by a monastic teaching order which claims unique spiritual powers. Eliade points out that Judaism and Christianity are distinguished from competitors by their more drastic historical sense.[13] Christianity claims to be in its own special way the fulfillment of the religious longings and needs of mankind. On this premise, its adherents ought not to reject, least of all in defensiveness, the widest possible study of the religions of mankind. It is not entirely utopian to expect that Eastern and Western philosophy may yet result in a new cultural synthesis comparable to that of Hebraism and Hellenism in Patristic thought. Western technology is already world-wide. At the same time, the need for a genuinely ecumenical Christian mission is self-evident.

It is impossible to understand the bases of Chinese culture apart from the ideas of Confucius. More a statesman and philosopher than a theologian, he nonetheless had a deep sense of the moral bases of human life. His interpretation set precedents for all of Chinese history which followed him. Religiously, Confucius' point of view was a timid one. He believed it necessary to learn of man before one can speak of deity. He understood himself as a teacher, looking to the past, and described his role as that of one who drew water out of a deep well. Yet in his own way he shaped tradition, but not in blind obedience. He found the basis for understanding reality in a universal moral norm. Those who violate the will of Heaven are in the end destroyed. Teaching and learning are the way of social reform. Confucius' program was more political than religious. Yet it was the opposite of all the opportunism of the time. Against dishonest politicians and ruthless rulers, he taught an abiding truth about life: Man must be true to his own nature. Tyrannical emperors persecuted Confucian scholars even to martyrdom, yet in the end their ideas were accepted and set a pattern for Chinese life. The strength of Confucianism lies in its humane optimism and moral common sense without utilitarianism. It is clear that in the end such a view alone did not meet the religious needs of the Chinese people. Their religious practice has been characterized by eclecticism; Confucianism, Taoism, a native Chinese religion, and Buddhism were accepted and taught together. It was Buddhism, coming from India in the first centuries of the Christian era, which brought a deep otherworldliness, a sense of mystery as well as a respect for human life.

The background of Buddhism lies in Hinduism, the national religion of the Indian sub-continent. In the sixth century before Christ, Gotama Buddha initiated a reform movement which carried such a dynamic as to become a world faith. Gotama sought a way of release from the cycles of rebirth in which he believed that man is enmeshed. His religious experience is summed up in the story of a chariot ride; whether it took place on a single day or over a longer period of time is not as important as its personal meaning.

The young prince saw first a diseased man, with running sores; then he passed an aged man who was leaning on a staff. He observed a corpse and finally a monk. Thus, sickness, old age and death as well as the way of salvation passed before him. Refusing riches and a career as a ruler, he left his native kingdom in quest of release from bondage and peace of soul. When he had at last achieved release and enlightment, he returned out of compassion to live among men and teach the way of salvation. The Buddhist cultus is preserved through a teaching order as well as through its holy books. Conceptually, it has a number of different forms, ranging from atheism to polytheism and even theism. Its principal divisions are Theravada, the more simple form practiced in Southeast Asia, and Mahayana, the inclusive vehicle. All adherents of the religion are united in the quest for Nirvana, release and bliss, an experience which has a place somewhat comparable to that of deity in Western theism. Assuredly, more than any other force in the Orient, Buddhism traditionally has brought compassion, peace and release. As a world religion, it transcends nation and race. Northrop has shown how much the civilization of East Asia—art, philosophy, modes of reflection and action as well as life attitudes—remains inexplicable apart from it.[14]

Hinduism is the world's largest living national faith. Like Japanese Shinto, it includes a large element of primitivism, but more than Shinto it has been modified by mature philosophical reflection. Really a family of religions, Hinduism contains a variety of conflicting ideas and claims to be non-credal. It has no founder, having grown up with the civilization in which it lives. For a time it yielded to Buddhism, only to return to dominance having been preserved by its hereditary priesthood. In fact, the two religions have enriched each other. Eclecticism is the basic mark of Eastern as compared with Western religious practice. Hinduism embraces pantheism as well as polytheism on the premise that

all life is divine; God and the soul are in the last reality
one and the same. An appearance-illusion theory of evil,
as well as a doctrine of rebirth, allows small concern for
history. Nevertheless, as a living faith, Hinduism continues
to provide the basis of belief of what Toynbee has identified as one of the major civilizations of mankind.[15] Gandhi,
who led the struggle against Western rule, was prepared to
borrow from Christianity, but not to accept its absolute faith
claims. Christianity, in fact, has brought increased moral sensitivity to India. However, Gandhi was revolted by the
Western practice of race discrimination, as well as by
caste in his own society. Fortunately, India has accepted
democracy and a secular state; thus a mutual exchange of
ideas and attitudes is possible.

The meeting of Hindu and Moslem in India, largely on
a communal basis, ended in riot, bloodshed and the parti-
tion of the sub-continent when it achieved independence
from Western rule. Approximately one out of seven of the
world's population accepts Mohammed's teachings as divine
revelation. Islam, obedience to God, prefers not to be known
by his name, since it regards him only as a prophet. Essentially a hot-land religion, Islam extends from the tip of
Western Africa, through the Middle East to Indonesia. Its
strong social structures have resisted penetration by Christianity better than those of any other major faith. For nearly
a millennium, its adherents were regarded as the major
threat to Christendom and resisted with force. When politically dominant, Islam allows freedom of worship but not
missionary propaganda to Judaism and Christianity; from
the outset, it has been characterized by a union of church
and state in theocracy. An unhappy legacy of hostility, ever
since the Crusades, prejudices the Moslem understanding
of Christianity. Fortunately, there are non-Christians as well
as Christians who desire a more objective and open understanding between the two religions. Certainly, it is inap-

propriate to omit the study of Islam from any survey of world civilizations.

The major world religions are the bearers of what H. Richard Niebuhr called internal history: historical meanings interpreted and reinterpreted in community memory.[16] As such, they determine life orientation. Should such ideas be added to the already growing confusion of religious notions in our society? The more practical question is whether it is possible to isolate education from them. Their holy books can be bought in paperback editions at every corner drug store. Critical appraisal cannot be developed if they are ignored in education. Too easily, they are approached romantically, as if the student could abandon his own historical background or presuppositions. Much less ought they to be considered with the intent of arriving at the lowest common denominator. The major world religions do not yield their most significant meanings on such superficial reading. Their richness ought not to be made a part of education unless one is prepared to give thoughtful, painstaking consideration. Yet their study does yield indispensable perspectives against the modern pseudo-religions as well as a secularism which considers faith to be irrelevant.

NOTES

1. Arnold Toynbee, *An Historian's Approach to Religion* (London: Oxford, 1956) and *Christianity Among the Religions of the World* (London: Oxford, 1958).
2. *Ibid.*
3. Dawson, *The Crisis of Western Education,* p. 147.
4. Henri Bergson, *The Two Sources of Morality and Religion* (New York: Doubleday Anchor, 1954).
5. Mircea Eliade, *Die Religionen und das Heilige, Elemente der Religiongeschichte* (Salzburg: Muller, 1954).
6. Bell, *op. cit.,* p. 128. Alfred North Whitehead, *Religion in the Making* (New York: Macmillan, 1926).
7. Karl Jaspers, *Vom Ursprung und Ziel der Geschichte* (Munich: Piper,

1950), pp. 25, 76. Cf. also *The Origin and Goal of History* (New Haven: Yale University Press, 1953).

8. Christopher Dawson, *The Dynamics of World History,* ed. John J. Mulloy (New York: Sheed and Ward, 1957), p. 119.

9. Hendrik Kraemer, *World Cultures and World Religions: The Coming Dialogue* (London: Lutterworth, 1960).

10. Küng calls attention to the interpretation of Paul Tillich. Cf. the latter's *Christianity and the Encounter of World Religions* (New York: Columbia University Press, 1963).

11. Karl Barth, *Kirchliche Dogmatik* (Zurich: Zollikon, 1948), 1/2, pp. 324-356. Cf. the American edition published by Scribner, *Church Dogmatics.*

12. Rudolf Otto, *The Idea of the Holy* (New York: Oxford University Press, 1950).

13. Mircea Eliade, *Cosmos and History,* tr. Willard R. Trask (New York: Harper, 1959), pp. 16of.

14. F. S. C. Northrop, *The Meeting of East and West* (New York: Macmillan, 1949), pp. 346–360.

15. Arnold Toynbee, *A Study of History.* Abridgement Vols. I–VI by D. C. Somervell (London: Oxford University Press, 1947), p. 244.

16. H. Richard Niebuhr, *The Meaning of Revelation* (New York: Macmillan, 1941).

15

The Jewish View

In contrast to the majority of Roman Catholic and Protestant leaders, many Jewish spokesmen have been especially critical of religion in public education. While there were Jewish parents who supported the Regents' Prayer in New York, the Jewish community as a whole continues to be suspicious of any common religious affirmation in the public schools. Except for a few Orthodox leaders, opinion against aid to parochial schools is virtually unanimous. Milton Himmelfarb, a contributing editor of the American Jewish Committee magazine *Commentary,* has remarked:

This is all the more striking because the central Jewish tradition clearly favors religious education and practice for non-Jews, provided their religion is not pagan. That tradition used to be as much a part of the popular consciousness as of the elite's learning.[1]

Himmelfarb recounts a story told to him as a boy by his mother, about a grandfather in the old country. A non-Jewish peasant coachman was engaged to drive the Jews to another town. After a few miles they passed a church, but

the driver did not cross himself. Grandfather waited for a
while and then on the pretext of having forgotten something,
told the driver to return home. He dismissed him when they
arrived at the house and explained to grandmother: "A
peasant who does not cross himself does not believe in God.
What is to prevent him from murdering me when we are
alone in the woods?"

What has happened in the American experience?[2] The
number of Jews living in the United States was only about
2,500 at the time of the revolution; by 1820, Jews numbered
some 5,000 in a population of 13,000,000. Later, immigration came in two waves. Between 1820–1870, it is estimated
that two to four hundred thousand Jews came to the United
States, largely from central Europe. They were often regarded as German Jews and encountered some of the same
resistance by the natives which met other immigrant groups.
Between 1870 and 1914, more than two million Jews immigrated to the United States, 80% from Russia, 20% from
the Austro–Hungarian Empire. This latter group remained
in the large cities, especially in the Eastern part of the
United States, living in what were in effect urban ghettos.
The religious background of the immigrants was either
orthodox, with a rabbi who was of little help in bridging
the gap to the new culture, or else they were secular adherents of ideologies of drastic change such as socialism.

Rabbi Arthur Gilbert, former National Director of the
Department of Inter-religious Cooperation of the Anti-
Defamation League, has commented that there "is no . . .
developed Jewish philosophy with regard to American
church-state issues."[3] The Jewish community, he asserts,
"has rested its case on secularistic and legalistic arguments. . . ." Whether this is a fair description must be judged
from positions taken in the discussion of public policy. As
a small minority, Jews do not wish their children to be
taught an alien faith. It is feared that most of the religion

included in public education will be predominately Christian. Himmelfarb emphasizes that present Jewish attitudes reflect the rather unified set of beliefs which has come into being since the Enlightenment and the beginning of civic equality.[4] In Europe, there was discrimination. In the United States, Jews have been attracted to the public schools positively because of the help which has come through them. The Jewish conviction is that the public schools are good and desirable in themselves. There is a general desire not to weaken them either in principle or in practice. The public schools have become a symbol of a benign, inclusive ideal; practically, they have been an instrument for individual progress which has enabled the Jewish citizen to move ahead with unexpected speed and completeness. Religious controversy is unwelcome and to be avoided.

Leo Pfeffer, Director of the American Jewish Congress Commission on Law and Social Action, describes the Jewish outlook as follows:

By the time Jews began coming to this country in substantial numbers at the turn of the twentieth century, the secularization of the public educational system had been completed. The overwhelming majority of Jews came from Czarist Russia and Poland. Jewish children fortunate enough to gain admittance to the government schools in those countries experienced daily the whiplash of official anti-Semitism and were never allowed to forget their inferior status. Moreover, the schools were pervaded with Christian teachings, ritual, and prayer, all of which the Jewish child had to endure in uncomplaining but unhappy silence.

When the Jewish immigrant came to America he found that the government school not only tolerated his child but actually welcomed him. He found too that his child was treated as the complete equal of all other children and that this equality of treatment was the proud boast of the school authorities. He found, finally, that except for some sporadic and often purely perfunctory reading of a few verses from the Bible, the schools were generally devoid of the Christological religiosity that so discomfited him in eastern Europe.[5]

Himmelfarb recounts addressing an adult study group at the request of his Rabbi, to explain why he believes some dominant Jewish attitudes on church-state matters are in need of revision. After Himmelfarb had spoken, a normally kind and friendly man rose to answer. He uttered only a few sentences, stopped and ran out of the room. The hearer later apologized for his outburst. Yet there was an explanation. Born and educated in Czechoslovakia, he had never forgotten the taunts and occasional beatings he suffered on the days when the clergy came to give religious instruction in the school.

Professor Joseph Blau of Columbia University in his *Story of Jewish Philosophy* comments that "the freedom of the Jew to practice his religion has never been abridged in the slightest degree" in the United States.[6] Rabbi Seymour J. Cohen has pointed out that the American Constitution represents the first time that such a basic document allowed for the full secular rights of Jewish citizens.[7] Today, Americans believe overwhelmingly that the Constitution is right in granting full equality to all citizens, irrespective of religious background and conviction. It would be an unthinkable abrogation of the national tradition if any alleged concern for moral and spiritual values would lead to discrimination against any part of the citizenry. The Supreme Court has understood that political and religious questions must remain separate. In fact, the separation of church and state has led to responsible interfaith contacts.

It is important to understand that the Jewish community has not reacted simply negatively or defensively to the American experience. Reformed and Conservative Judaism have modified religious practice and belief in their respective ways. Conditions have not been the same as in Eastern

Europe. There is a fundamentally new spirit of acceptance in the national community in spite of limited barriers. Herberg finds that whereas the second generation moved toward secularism, the third generation has returned to its Jewish roots.[8] The old national sense is gone. A new religious interest and concern to find one's own identity and life meaning has emerged. There is a desire to be accepted as part of American society, but as Jews.

The issue in education is not just theological but cultural: The Jewish community memory of persecution dates from pre-Christian times. Judaism is the parent religion; Christianity had its beginnings in part in revolt against it. Christians did not at once separate themselves from the synagogue, but claimed to be the new Israel. Early Christian preaching affirmed that Jesus was the promised Messiah. When converts were not Jews, they often came from Gentiles who had been predisposed to monotheism under Jewish influence. The earliest Christian proclamation, addressed to Jews rather than to Gentiles, was careful to guard against any unrestricted assertion of guilt for the crucifixion. In a later period, as the Gentile Christians were separated from "the Jews," they were portrayed increasingly as a group hostile to the truth. The pattern of using the state against a differing religious conviction was not new with Christians. Jews from the first century persecuted Christians and on occasion participated in Roman repression against the new religion. However, following the fall of Jerusalem, the Jewish community in Palestine and Persia seems to have had little close contact with the heresy. There are only a few negative references to Christianity in the Talmud. Maurer in *Kirche und Synagogue (Church and Synagogue)* points out that such apologists as Justin Martyr and Tertullian wrote against a stereotyped Jewish point of view more than to really living opponents.[9]

The modern historian may be amazed at how little real

appreciation there was of Jewish tradition by Christians, much less concern for social justice or the rights of man. The dominant Christian image of Judaism was that of an untrue, even accursed religion. In the Jewish community, a negative view of the cross had been evoked by charges of collective guilt as well as by politically imposed conversions. Forced baptism can be dated from at least 558 A.D. Certainly, one can overstate the direct conflict between the church and synagogue in the medieval period; all controlling factors were not religious. Yet it is not hard to understand why Jews often fear that a renewed Christian theological interest will have negative potentialities for Jewish life and culture. Christians expected state favor following the conversion of Constantine. Early Christian emperors who attempted to maintain full legal equality of religions met strong resistance. Later, it was convenient for secular rulers and knights to loot Jewish property. More than once, it was only the Biblical word that a remnant of Jews would endure until the end of time which allowed their continued life in the midst of persecution.

The Reformation did not bring emancipation, as many Protestants have wanted to believe. Luther like Mohammed at first spoke in friendly terms of the Jews, seeking their conversion to Christianity. When their century-long traditions failed to yield to his new ideas, he discouraged any Christian contact with them and even called for punishment by death of the rabbis. Tolerance came with the era of the French Revolution in Western Europe. For Judaism, in particular, religious freedom brought new problems and adjustments. Changing political conceptions and world views forced it to undertake re-evaluations similar to those which Roman Catholicism and Protestantism had been making since the Renaissance. In the relative isolation and self-containment of the pre-modern world, traditional orthodoxy could avoid major confrontation with nationalism and

modern science. Such was no longer the case following emancipation. Only with great difficulty and the threat of obscurantism could Jewish learning any longer be confined
to the world of the Torah and Talmud; it reacted either
defensively or in accommodation. Earlier communalism had
been built on religious divisions. Enlightenment ideologies
of freedom and concern for the rights of all men were premised on belief in a universal reason which transcends credal
differences.

Enlightenment ideas reached the mass of the Jewish population only slowly. Their most advanced form can be seen
in the writings of Moses Mendelssohn (1729–1786). It was
this Jewish friend of Lessing who inspired his famous drama
advocating tolerance, explained by the figure of three rings.
Mendelssohn in *Jerusalem,* written in 1783, urged his fellow
believers to open themselves to the larger cultural community. Complying with the laws of the country, they were
to continue to adhere to the faith of their forefathers. The
influence of the Enlightenment is most evident in the way
in which Mendelssohn valued reason over tradition. Unlike
medieval apologists, he did not try to work out a detailed
defense of Jewish principles as compared with Moslem or
Christian ideas. Rather, he regarded the Jewish Bible as
supplementing universal principles of knowledge. This attitude continued to dominate much of non-orthodox Jewish
interpretation throughout the nineteenth century. It appears, for example, in the writings of Hermann Cohen
(1842–1918), a leading Jewish intellectual who was at the
same time an outstanding Kantian philosopher. In the *Religion of Reason on the Basis of Jewish Sources,* he described
Jewish faith in terms of ethical autonomy and the unity of
God.

At present, Jewish religious thought has reacted against
Enlightenment perspectives in the face of the cultural crises
of the time. Judaism is not regarded as part of a larger

whole. Instead, there is an attempt to recover personal "roots" in its particular point of view. The new mood had its profound theological expression during the period of the two world wars in such thinkers as Franz Rosenzweig and Martin Buber.[10] Rosenzweig wrote part of his principal work on army regulation postcards, while serving as a German soldier during the First World War. Rejecting eclecticism, he argued that reason alone is inadequate apart from tradition and personal faith. The particularity of Judaism as a historical religion cannot be compromised. "I am wholly Jewish," Rosenzweig wrote, protesting against a secularized, rationalized environment. Both Rosenzweig and Martin Buber grew up in a situation of emancipation but reacted against it. Emancipation seemed to Rosenzweig to have been a disaster. In the ghetto, the Jew had his own land and community. Later, all was in confusion. Buber's "I-Thou" interpretation sought to overcome the impersonalized, desacralized world. Modern life lacks organic community, he protested; wholeness can be achieved only in personhood, not in thinghood. Whereas Rosenzweig died before the Hitler debacle, Buber immigrated to the new State of Israel where Judaism can be expressed as an inclusive way of life and culture.

For Judaism, the problem has not only been one of intellectual reorientation, but overt persecution. Today, Judaism is established in Israel. The early Zionist leaders found little support among Western Jewry which felt secure in pre-world war Europe. The Nazi attempt to destroy the entire people brought the Zionist ideal to realization in the founding of the State of Israel. No doubt, the rebirth of Jewish national hopes has encouraged cultural consciousness. Of course, Jewish opinion in the United States is non-Zionist as well as Zionist, secular as well as religious. Movements such as Reconstructionism have hoped to unite a variety of points of view—orthodox, conservative and reformed—in the conviction that Judaism must express its own authentic culture. It cannot allow itself to become just another American denomination. When Rabbi Mordecai Kaplan, the founder of Reconstructionism, speaks of Judaism as a civilization, he does not mean to limit it to the State of Israel.[11] On the contrary, he is emphatic in urging that Jews in the United States accept the world of American democracy fully. It is the glory of democracy that it allows the Jew to retain his identity.

Equal rights is a civic and legal arrangement; its effective implementation depends on conviction which in practice will refuse discrimination. The renewal of persecution with the rise of the modern totalitarian state—Nazi or Communist—has made doubly clear the danger of lawlessness which perennially threatens beneath an apparently calm surface. Persecution has its deepest roots in the evil from which the high religions seek deliverance. Hatred is not overcome alone by political measures, much less by mere expressions of good will. Is the safest strategy a completely secular public life with religious communalism? The question remains: What are to be the motivations for responsible citizenship in a secular society? How is it to be kept from becoming "demonic" or idolatrous as in modern totalitarianism? Communalism carries its own dangers of misunderstanding.

Jewish misgivings about cooperation with Christians, even in a democratic state, should not come as a surprise after centuries of intolerance and persecution. More often than not, the adherents of both religions have regarded each other defensively. Christians have viewed the Jews, popularly at least, as those who have rejected the Messiah. Jews have looked at Christians as those who imposed innovations in unfaithfulness to the Law of God and monotheism. The conflict between the two religions has been understood from these stereotypes. Until the eighteenth century, Jewish-Christian relations were based on the pattern of communalism which is still found throughout the Middle East today. Christianity was supported by the state. However, it would be a mistake to suppose that contacts between Jews and Christians were always as restricted as in the late medieval ghetto. Before the Crusades, there had been major intellectual exchange between Jews, Christians and Moslems. The effort to unify Christendom against the Turk led to new pressures against the Jewish minority. Following the French Revolution, the pattern of communalism has broken down with the recognition that the rights of citizenship transcend confessional lines. Disestablishment assuredly changed the basis of interfaith relations. Judaism is no longer a social unity, as in the segregation of the medieval period. It entered a new period of readjustment which continues until the present.

Pfeffer attributes the present secularization of public education to an alliance of Protestants and secular humanists, supported by the Jewish minority.[12] Whereas continued support for the alliance is uncertain among Protestants, the majority of Jewish opinion adheres to it strongly. The Synagogue Council of America together with the National Community Relations Advisory Council in 1957 issued a statement on the place of religion in public education as approved by "major rabbinic, congregational and community relations organizations." The preamble of the pronouncement acknowledges that

The American democratic system is founded in large part upon ethical and moral concepts derived from the great religions of mankind. The preservation and fostering of these concepts are essential to the fullest realization of the American ideal and their growth and development as major forces in American life should be the deep concern of every citizen.

The statement holds further:

The maintenance and furtherance of religion are the responsibilities of the synagogue, the church and the home, and not the public school system; the utilization in any manner of the time, facilities, personnel, or funds of the public school system for purposes of religious instruction should not be permitted. Insofar as the teaching of "spiritual values" may be understood to signify religious teaching, this must remain as it has been the responsibility of the home, the church and the synagogue. Insofar as it is understood to signify the teaching of morality, ethics and good citizenship, a deep commitment to such values has been successfully inculcated by our public schools in successive generations of Americans. The public schools must continue to share responsibility for fostering a commitment to these moral values, without presenting or teaching any sectarian or theological sources or sanctions for values. The public schools must and should teach with full objectivity the role that religion has played in the life of mankind and in the development of society, when such teaching is intrinsic to the regular subject matter being studied. We are opposed to attempts by the public elementary and secondary schools to go beyond this, and teach about the *doctrines* of religion. Without passing upon the question of whether or not such teaching is inconsistent with the principle of the separation of church and state, we believe that factual, objective and impartial teaching about the doctrines of religion is an unattainable objective. Any attempt to introduce such teaching into the public schools poses the grave threat of pressures upon school personnel from sectarian groups and compromises the impartiality of teaching and the integrity of the public educational system. Our opposition to such teaching rests on these grounds. . . . We submit, moreover, that attempts at religious inculcation in the public schools, even of articles of faith drawn from all religions and endorsed by representatives of all, violate the traditional American principle of separation of church and state.[13]

Is this all that can be said on Jewish premises? Few contemporary thinkers have been as concerned with the problem of Jewish adjustment to the modern world view as the founder of the Reconstructionist Movement, Rabbi Mordecai Kaplan.[14] His own interpretation of religion is probably too naturalistic to gain majority Jewish acceptance. Yet his commentary on Jewish problems of alienation from tradition as well as the difficulties of adjustment to the contemporary world, remains valuable. According to Rabbi Kaplan, the problem of reconstruction is not just theological, but sociological and psychological. The movement he leads seeks to transcend theological differences, encouraging Jews of various convictions to continue to work together. His own career has exemplified characteristic problems of readjustment. Serving as Rabbi of an orthodox congregation, he found the position he represented increasingly unacceptable in the light of his own historical and philosophical study. While he was considering vocational re-orientation, he was asked to become leader of the Teachers' Institute at Jewish Theological Seminary. Feeling deeply the need to give Judaism relevance to the lives of modern people, he developed the Reconstructionist program.

Kaplan regards the Reformed, Conservative and Orthodox schools of Judaism (he distinguishes Orthodoxy from traditional Judaism as anti-Reform) as all belonging to the "Greater Judaism in the Making." Sociologically, reaction to modernity has produced two extremes. On the one hand, there is the assimilationist who wishes to give up all signs of Jewishness; he even resents his own Jewish heritage and the limits which it imposes upon him. On the other hand, there are Jews who suppose that they can live in an exclusively Hebrew world. Kaplan believes that Jewish life can be reintegrated only as it is recognized that Judaism is not primarily a sect or a party but a civilization. There must be revitalization of Jewish community life in the face of discrimination. Only by being himself culturally can the Jew contribute fully to the modern world. For example, language and art need to be recovered. Such a view is the antithesis of the earlier Enlightenment faith in universal reason. It is only one expression of the attempt—by no means limited to Reconstructionism—to recover personal "roots" in Judaism.

To be sure, others are less concerned than Kaplan that the community should not serve religion but religion the community. Yet the problem of interreligious relations remains. Of course, Kaplan is correct in holding that the Jews would have long since perished if they had been only another minority! Essentially, their uniqueness is not simply racial but religious. Pfeffer judges discerningly that problems of interreligious relations would continue even if racial discrimination were fully eliminated in the United States! Kaplan shares with other Jewish leadership the desire that the public schools shall not teach Christianity. Yet his writings do not accept the view that it is completely impossible to teach about religion in state-supported institutions. He encourages Jewish historical study under the norms of modern criticism rather than the Torah interpretation of the past.

Here the purpose is to enlarge the cultural horizon of the student. In that spirit, the teaching of the Bible would be possible even in a public high-school or college. It would be foolish to discourage that kind of instruction, on the ground that it is not only untraditional but completely neutral, from the standpoint of Jewish life. Better by far to have that kind of instruction than none. Thousands of Jewish children, who now remain abysmally ignorant of the Bible, could in that way acquire some knowledge of it.[15]

Kaplan recognizes that Christianity has had an indispensable role in raising Western man above the level of the barbarian. Like other developed religions, it supplies the ethical insights necessary to the civilization in which it lives.

Apart from such help, the threat of irresponsibility and totalitarianism remains. Judaism can only meet its own constituency's need. Kaplan's evaluation of its contribution is assuredly a sound one:

> The main emphasis, however, when the Bible is taught nowadays must be on what it should mean to us, in view of the elements in our environment which constitute a serious challenge to Jewish life. Those elements are: modern nationalism, modern scientism and the acceptance of force as the final arbiter in human affairs. Each of these three modern developments is a menace to the existence of the Jewish people. . . . It is the duty of the Jewish teacher so to interpret the Bible as to enable the child when he grows up, to withstand the impact of these three tendencies upon his life as a Jew in the modern world.[16]

If we concede that the democratic way of life is in need of religious sanctions, it follows that we have to reconsider the relations of state and church in the area of education, in which both claim an interest and a right to exercise control. . . . It has been tacitly assumed that the denominational churches could take care of their religious orientation and ethical adjustment. That tacit understanding is no longer satisfactory either to educators or to churchmen. . . . *Some religious faith must underlie all normative teaching, even of the so-called secular subjects.* Moreover, to entrust exclusively to denominational schools the teaching of religion exposes the American public to divisive influences that complicate, to say the least, the creation of that spiritual unity which must prevail in America, if democracy is to work.

So much for the point of view of the educator. To the religionist, the silence of the public schools on religion is, in effect, if not in intent, a depreciation of the importance of religion, at least of its importance to American life. The public schools teach loyalty to the state, for that has always been conceived as the justification of the state's interest in the school. But loyalty to the state, without loyalty to a universal God, leads directly to that apotheosis of the state which is the very essence of fascism.

It can thus be seen that education for democracy involves a problem which, far from having been solved, has grown more complicated with the years. Various attempts have been made to cope with the problem, ranging all the way from state support of denominational education to the release of an hour of public school time to be used, under church auspices, for religious education of public school children. All of these measures have been hastily conceived. They hardly scratch the surface of the problem. They are not based on a sound philosophy of religion. Without such a philosophy, it is impossible to assess properly the fundamental issues involved in the relationship between church and state, as it affects the process of education.[17]

The case for the Christian study of Judaism is simple enough: Judaism is the parent religion, however modified or disclaimed. It is important that the Church should hear the voice of Jewish faith, expressed by its own teachers and on its own premises. On the other hand, the modern Jew confronts a culture which does not have exclusively secular roots. For good or ill, it is influenced by Christianity. It seems dubious whether there can be a simply neutral meeting between Jews and Christians. Fortunately, there are today opportunities for a renewed and creative encounter between their religions on the basis of new Biblical studies. The Dominican scholar, Bernard Lambert, describes the Bible as the best meeting place for such diverse points of view.[18] The insights of Biblical research are not simply sectarian, but grounded in the history of religion. It is our conviction that Jews and Christians have a unique opportunity to contribute lasting new dimensions to education. But this is not possible unless they are willing to encourage open, undefensive search for the deepest faith insights of their respective traditions. Much depends on larger community relations between the adherents of the two traditions.

Fundamental is the question of whether the decisive encounter between Judaism and Christianity is to be one of
culture or of faith. Is faith to have priority over, and indeed
judge, culture for adherents of both religions? Of course,
the two dimensions of religious life cannot be separated as
much as some sectarian Protestants have supposed. If a re-
ductionistic or pragmatic interpretation of religion is accepted in education, Judaism and Christianity can be understood to face each other as one culture against another. One's
particular tradition, with its community loyalties, is affirmed
as a whole and defended in a fight for survival. Or, is the
encounter to be with faith? In the latter case, likeness and
difference can be affirmed in a common theism which will
not expect the complete exclusion of religion from education. Differences can be tolerated because God and not culture is the last reference! A monotheism which really pro-
claims faith in the one God as judge and redeemer, will
need the widest possible intellectual perspectives to do justice to complex issues. If the Jewish platform—as is too often
the case in Protestantism—is for a simply secular common
life, its implications for education should not be described
as "religious." Secularism is a faith which contends with
other faiths, but in the end limits the dynamic of religion.

Of course, the Jewish position cannot be determined
apart from responsible leadership within its own community.
Fortunately, there are at least the beginnings of re-evaluation
in terms of present needs and problems. Rabbi Seymour
Siegel of the Jewish Theological Seminary has spoken out
in an important commentary on "Church and State." [19]
Rabbi Siegel emphasizes that originally there was no secular
society or education, only Jewish and Christian communities,
the former to be sure in the ghetto. Historically, the separation of church and state developed in the attempt to restore
peace following the wars of religion. In Western Europe, it
was encouraged by the rationalistic philosophy of the En-

lightenment. Classical Judaism knows no such doctrine; instead, it sees the state as the creation of the divine imperative. It rejects in principle the separation of religion from culture. "The political philosophy of Judaism might be summed up in these words: the state is a legitimate and necessary part of human life. . . . However, the rights of the state are circumscribed by the Law of God." [20] How is this position to be expressed in a pluralistic society which practices separation of church and state?

Secularism may be a necessary and even desirable social arrangement in a pluralistic order. One ought not to be deceived into believing that it supplies the moral axioms necessary either to democracy or tolerance. Such axioms are not self-evident, much less derived from science. Rabbi Siegel cites the Jewish theologian, Martin Buber, in emphasizing the importance of faith in the formation of a society. Buber argued that all culture, including its political systems, is built on some central core of affirmations concerning the nature of reality and the imperatives of life which flow from these affirmations. This tradition in the Western world has been Jewish-Christian. The religious idea is the cement which holds culture together. It was only certain extreme forms of Enlightenment thought which advocated an atheistic society and placed organized religions at the level of private clubs. Judaism does not allow that religion can be a simply private affair. It seeks to bring the individual into a right relation with his God through loving obedience and through responsible action in the world. "Unless the ethos of society is permeated with the recognition of a transcendent reality and a justice beyond human justice, we are all in danger." [21]

Why, Rabbi Siegel asks, does Jewish opinion so often favor completely secular policy in society at large? It is his position that Judaism like Christianity premises a transcendent source of value and reality. This claim cannot be given up or limited to private life. However, Jews cannot be expected to forget that they fared best in the nineteenth century under "secular," "lay" or even anti-religious governments which deliberately sought to remove all influence of religion from public life. Now, the alleged benevolence of such governments has been given the lie in the twentieth century. Possessed with their own power, they have denied not only the transcendent judgment of God, but the rights of man.

Both Judaism and Christianity affirm that society is in need of prophetic criticism from the point of view of higher values. Religion is not identical with culture. Naturally, religion can be used simply as a defense of the status quo. Yet it ought not to be without influence on the ethos of the national life. Public recognition of religion is no substitute for faith. Yet, without it, the culture tends to believe in itself as its own last end; traditional ideas and symbols become irrelevant. The public school teacher who must remain completely silent about belief in God cannot explain to students why the Declaration of Independence espouses inalienable rights with which men are endowed by their creator. What about the rights of those persons who do not believe in God, which the Supreme Court has been so careful to protect? Negative freedom to criticize should not be allowed to preclude all opportunities for positive religious expression. "Any absolutist view of the relationship between religion and the state in the United States—over and above its constitutional and legal requirements—is neither true to the spirit of America and the consensus upon which it is built, nor is it good public policy." [22]

Rabbi Siegel points out that there has been positive gain in the separation of church and state. Yet sound principles can be taken to extremes as in Justice Douglas' proposal that all religious influence be taken away from government. In fact, American society has been built on a particular consensus which extends beyond any one sectarian group. Rabbi Siegel quotes Father John Courtney Murray, "The consensus is come to by the people; they become a people by coming to it." Rabbi Siegel accepts the position of President John Bennett of Union Theological Seminary: the state is neutral as between the traditional faiths, but is not indifferent to the religious life of its citizens, or to the relevance of religion to its affairs. Although it cannot teach religion, it does use religious symbols and provide for common recognition of the Reality which religious agencies alone have the competence to interpret. It is in this context that the Supreme Court's defense of secular political structures has been most important as against religious partisanship. However, removal of all forms of religious symbolism—prayers, proclamations, invocations of the Deity—from public life ought not to be accepted complacently by organized religion; the sovereignty of God is in danger of being denied!

It is no longer fair to say that the religion of the public schools is a "nondescript, syncretistic Protestantism"! B. I. Bell has come unhappily too close to the truth: "At present all religions except one are in practice negated and that one religion is given monopoly care." On this view, the religion of the public schools is a non-theistic patriotic secularism. Such a situation has come about in part because members of the three major groups have insisted on absolutistic rather than provisional solutions to the problem of religion in education. A rigid attitude on the part of each religious confession brings havoc on the school system. Jewish leaders have sometimes argued against religion in public education on the grounds that children will be made more conscious of the differences between Jews and Gentiles. Rabbi Siegel urges that Jews should not attempt to create a desacralized culture in which all separation is erased. The first to be converted in a post-Jewish, post-Gentile milieu, he believes, will be the Jews who in rejection of legitimate distinction can only dig their own grave. Authentic religion with differences, not a bland common Americanism in which all parties look alike, belongs rightly to American public life. There is a narrow ridge to walk between rigid doctrinairism and denial of religious freedom. Rabbi Siegel concludes that the risk is worth taking. The universe does have a center of meaning and education must speak of it! "I hope I am not exaggerating when I say that nothing less than the fate of our society is at stake." [23]

NOTES

1. *Commonweal,* Vol. 79, No. 18 (January 31, 1964), p. 524.
2. Herberg, *op. cit.,* p. 186.
3. Arthur Gilbert, "Religion in the Public School—A New Approach to the Jewish Position," *Religious Education* (July-August, 1961), pp. 297ff., 301.
4. Himmelfarb, *op. cit.*
5. Leo Pfeffer, *Creeds in Competition: A Creative Force in American Culture* (New York: Harper, 1958), pp. 59–60.
6. Joseph Blau, *The Story of Jewish Philosophy* (New York: Random House, 1962), p. 286.
7. Seymour J. Cohen, "Religious Freedom and the Constitution," *Conservative Judaism,* XVII, No. 3–4 (1963), pp. 13–38.
8. Herberg, *op. cit.,* p. 201.
9. Wilhelm Maurer, *Kirche und Synagogue* (Stuttgart: Kohlhamer, 1953).
10. Martin Buber and Franz Rosenzweig, *Die Schrift und ihre Verdeutschung* (Berlin: Schocken, 1936). Martin Buber, *Israel and the World: Essays in a Time of Crisis* (New York: Schocken, 1948). Simon Noveck, ed., *Great Jewish Thinkers of the Twentieth Century* (Clinton, Mass.: Colonial Press, 1963).
11. Mordecai Kaplan, *Judaism as a Civilization: Toward a Reconstruction of American Jewish Life* (New York: Yoseloff, 1957).
12. Pfeffer, *op. cit.,* pp. 41–42.
13. New York, 1957.
14. Mordecai Kaplan, *The Greater Judaism in the Making: A Study of the Modern Evolution of Judaism* (New York: Reconstructionist Press, 1960).
15. Mordecai Kaplan, *The Future of the American Jew* (New York: Macmillan, 1948), p. 450.
16. Kaplan, *op. cit.,* p. 456. Cf. also *Judaism as a Civilization,* p. 550.
17. Kaplan, *The Future of the American Jew, op. cit.,* pp. 510–511.

18. Lambert, *op. cit.*, pp. 247–264.
19. Seymour Siegel, "Church and State," *Conservative Judaism*, XVII, No. 3–4 (1963), 1–12.
20. *Ibid.*, p. 5.
21. *Ibid.*, p. 8.
22. *Ibid.*, p. 6.
23. *Ibid.*, pp. 11–12.

16

Science and Religion

More than any other force, scientific discovery has changed man's life in recent centuries; it continues to do so even more radically in the space age. As Theodor Litt points out, it is a spiritual force of great power with inevitable consequences for education.[1] Scientific method is the vital dynamic in the explosion of knowledge in a host of different fields. Objective study of the history and methods of science —what it is and does as well as how it has grown—is imperative for any genuinely modern education. Not just knowledge about, but participation in scientific disciplines is required. Institutional religion, often too busy with its own tasks and sectarian conflicts, has not given enough attention or support to this area of scholarship. Interconfessional cooperation seems inevitable in any real concern for the new problems presented by modern science and technology.

The impact of natural science on education is to be welcomed and encouraged. Practically, it means more rigorous standards of instruction as well as an emphasis on critical thought and logic. However, there is also the danger that science will become an ideology which replaces humanistic and religious interests; such a development threatens to come about from practical pressures more than from any deliberate strategy. In fact, the earlier conflict between science and religion, so prominent in the discussion of evolution, is now largely past. Outstanding scientists continue to affirm that their research cannot invalidate religion; instead, its moral insight is needed for the right use of new discoveries. Physicists associated with research on the atomic bomb have been especially sensitive to their personal responsibility in relation to modern warfare.

Science in the limited modern sense is one horizon of knowledge, a particular method of arriving at a given type of understanding. It cannot tell us what it means to exist as persons. Personal relations yield themselves to scientific measurement only in limited degree; human beings are qualitative as well as quantitative. Natural science gives us reports of the world about us, but these reports are the work of man's self-initiative and judgment. Most of all, science cannot reduce personality to determinism. There is no social physics! We ought not to expect science to supply a mathematical equation or new chemical element that will solve all the problems of education. Indeed, the principle of unbroken continuity, so often invoked in support of mechanism, has now been re-evaluated and modified in terms of an indeterminacy principle. Scientific method, no more than a particular form of government, democratic or otherwise, cannot take man beyond the limits of a particular world view, much less his finitude. Most assuredly, it does not prove that "nature is all." The revolution in physics which has taken place in this century has made clear more than ever that scientific method cannot solve philosophical and religious issues involved in the problem of transcendence and the existence of God.

It is sometimes supposed that the new scientific knowledge and technique which makes possible space exploration

will also solve man's moral problems. The evidence is to
the contrary. The wonderful technology necessary to carry
men to another planet is not a chance development, but the
fruit of intelligence in the careful planning of many men
and governments. Science is the product of human purpose
which it cannot by itself supply. The risks of space flight
make doubly clear how precarious and fragile is the new
epoch-making human achievement. Not automatic, its success requires intent, will and decision exercised in freedom.
The scientist must seek to know the truth and adhere to it
in good conscience. If his integrity is corrupted, science suffers loss. More than this, his work is not fully predetermined.
New discoveries require imagination and creativity which in
turn presuppose freedom.

We may evaluate our present educational achievement by
asking what our civilization would have to offer in a visit
to another planet. The "earth scientists" expect to put a man
on the moon within a decade, or failing that, at least by
the end of the century. Exploration of the other planets in
our solar system is expected to follow. The question remains: What sort of person will we "export"? Our situation
is in some respects similar to that of the first European set-
tlers in the Americas. The "newcomers" as invaders brought
positive help: the horse, new crops, science and religion.
However, they were responsible for abuse as well: slavery
came with the Europeans. Indian civilization was destroyed
in Mexico and Peru. We must ask whether the "earth men"
will do better in their new exploration. Will they make life
more free and worthwhile in other places, or only spread
atomic destruction over an interplanetary realm?

The new frontiers require that education go beyond
technology and raise fundamental questions about man
himself. The mysteries of the atom may be simple compared
with those of human choice and imagination. We are not
confronted by other persons just as things, but by the fact

of freedom. When "earth man" is at last on his way to other planets, he will still have reason to marvel at the richness of personality as well as the order of the universe. If he has never understood that it is they which together make possible his travel, the trip will hardly have been worth the making.

Bernard Iddings Bell in a characteristically provocative remark commented that persons who argue for religion in public education have come to occupy a place comparable to the advocates of the teaching of science, a generation ago.[2] Formerly, the curriculum was restricted by a lack of scientific information. Now, it is religion which is left out with a consequent truncation of knowledge. Education cannot avoid asking about the relation between the two fields; care must be taken to avoid oversimplification of either. Too often, naturalistic views of education have encouraged the stereotype that science deals only with fact and religion with unverifiable speculation. But science is not simply a collection of facts; it has an indispensable theoretical component. In practice, it is highly symbolic, studded with abstract, often mathematical, models in new dimensions of theory. Its name has often been invoked far beyond any legitimate usage by persons who are not practicing scientists.

The philosopher Karl Jaspers has raised the question of whether modern science gives any inclusive scientific world view in isolation from history and philosophy.[3] Assuredly, exact observation and mathematical formulation are required. The individual sciences represent a critical appraisal of knowledge—by experiment and reflection—in a particular field. Yet, according to Jaspers, they do not of themselves bring a unified or complete view of reality. Natural science is an attempt to find verifiable answers to particular problems. Individual sciences develop their methodologies in relation to their data. Indeed, it belongs to scientific method that it recognize its own limits; otherwise it cannot be em-

ployed critically. The modern scientific enterprise has
brought new principles of interpretation, but these are not
exhaustive. Jaspers recognizes the danger of speaking of
science as if it were a universal or finished whole which
could be imposed on all types of experience, aesthetic, moral
and religious. Instead, he maintains that it is without
moral norms; this fact poses the danger of nihilism. He is emphatic in affirming that education must reinstate the larger
intellectual legacy of Western history, Hebrew-Christian as
well as Greco-Roman. Otherwise, ours is a rootless culture
which will inevitably ignore the deepest bases of human
freedom in the inner life of man. Scientific "authority" is no
substitute for philosophy or religion.

Naturalistic educational theory developed its own type
of scientism in alleged dependence on biological evolution.
Universal norms were disavowed. Values were described in
terms of their origins. Nature was reduced to what happens
or is useful without any intrinsic order of reality. Such reductionism inevitably confused what is with what ought to
be. A minimum philosophical insight requires that one
distinguish more carefully between the descriptive and the
normative as well as the empirical and the rational. No
doubt, the pragmatists were in revolt against Hegel's abstract
intellectualism. Yet they failed to understand that science
is perspectival and not all-encompassing. Nature became an
even more mysterious reference than deity! Not only was
science reduced to a trial-and-error chronicle; freedom and
morality remain unexplained. Out of his native goodness
and armed with scientific method, modern man was to remake history without reference to tradition or authority.
But are technological and personal moral development really
analogous? The question is not the sincerity of the claim that
science will sustain personal moral growth and progress. It
is rather whether such a view does not represent a superficial

stereotype which is in fact an escape from difficult moral decisions.

Naturalism is not a radically new philosophy. The basic principles of this outlook were appraised by Socrates and Plato before the Christian epoch. Their rejection of its basic claims can help the modern observer to see it in larger perspective. Part of the present difficulty in educational theory arises from a lack of philosophical reference. Increasingly, modern scientific method retreats from inclusive metaphysical explanation, regarding its constructs as functional. The physical sciences especially rely on mathematical abstraction. They attempt to encompass particular events in abstract laws. Historical existence is generalized as much as possible in inclusive categories. The question remains whether this abstraction represents all of reality. Can human responsibility and freedom be replaced by it any more than by an earlier mechanism or determinism? Of course, such scientific analysis is not simply timeless, but set in a context of development as part of the historical life of man. In short, much of it is the history of science.

The risks and responsibility of human freedom break through again and again in scientific analysis. The human person simply will not reduce to a technique or thing. Freedom and responsibility are presupposed by modern research. Highly specialized, the latter requires the cooperative effort of many inquirers in a common quest for truth. Its genius is one of the combined personal discipline, sensitivity, insight and creativity of a larger community of specialists. Science is not a predetermined whole any more than great art. The intelligence and sense of obligation which underly it point to man's remarkable capacity for moral development. Its very human interpretation and quest presuppose order rather than chaos, freedom rather than determinism. Where will its worthy human achievement, made in such high purpose and creativity, lead us at last? Technology can be used by totalitarian states to further their own ends, indeed to strengthen empire. We must look in another direction before we can even begin to resolve the human dilemmas which continue to multiply with its expansion.

Little positive help or meaning is forthcoming from the claim that freedom and intelligence are just cosmic accidents; this is not science at all! It is, in fact, no explanation whatever to assert that order, intelligence or morality happen by chance. It is nonsense to speak of good and evil as questions of organic evolution alone. Conscience and freedom interrupt and even reverse organic processes; thought and will are more than instinct. The attempt to comprehend man in natural processes, as if they were all-inclusive, is clearly contrary to the facts. Most dangerous of all, perhaps, is the claim that the species moves ever upward and onward: we need not be overly concerned about conscience or morality. But "upward and onward" is in itself a thinly veiled judgment of good and evil. It has little or no meaning if there are no unique persons with an abiding sense of right and wrong.

The deterministic claim is still invoked as "scientific." We know for certain, it is said, that man's intellect is a product of his conditioning. Men act exclusively from their environment and training. Caught in a pattern of long-standing habits and dispositions, they cannot change but must do this or that. The remark of a college student who had just begun his first course in psychology summarizes this judgment: "All the world is determined by chance." Of course, if this were the case we should have great difficulty in knowing it because knowledge is more than chance. Education would be impossible. The recall from "scientism" has been sharp in recent decades. Biologists now recognize that it is an abuse of their science to invoke its method or findings to prove that we live in a meaningless world. A more realistic examination of the human situation leads to the understanding that the events of personal life do not happen automatically. Man thinks and decides with intelligence. Unlike the animals, he is not bound simply to instinct, but reflects and decides as a historical being caught up in a host of conditions and circumstances.

Today, there is little danger that science will be unhonored in education. The real problem is whether science will be reduced to technology and not set in its larger context as part of the intellectual and spiritual life of man. The distinguished English mathematician and physicist, Alfred North Whitehead, made a major contribution to educational theory by his inclusive philosophical insights. Whitehead spent the last decades of his life in the United States as a professor of Harvard University. Earlier with Bertrand Russell, he was co-author of *Principia Mathematica;* subsequently, his philosophical ideas developed in the opposite direction from those of Russell. In collected essays entitled, *The Aims of Education,* Whitehead insists repeatedly that the perspectives of teaching must be not only technical and scientific, but also moral and religious.[4] Without question, he would recognize that exclusion of religion from so much of public education has left the curriculum basically unbalanced. Whitehead regarded morality and religion not simply as particular systems of thought, but as bringing a quality of life and insight without which education becomes barren.

Whitehead did not accept the empiricist position that science and education together can develop their own standards of measurement simply by looking about at the world. He would reply that such a view begs the question. There must be a point of beginning in critical reflection and explicit presuppositions. His famous comment was that all Western philosophy has been a footnote to the ideas of Plato. Whitehead's contribution was one of relating modern scientific discovery, especially relativity and quantum mechanics, to the Western intellectual tradition and restoring a sound hierarchy of aims, goals and values as against modern reductionism and naturalism.

Whitehead was simply arguing from a larger cultural tradition when he affirmed that the meaning of science and technology—the two not being the same—must be set in the full context of human intelligence and community. Scientific meanings are not simply arbitrary abstraction but related to an order or reality which carries lasting structures. Whitehead insisted that nature is neither mechanism or idea; against this "bifurcation" he strongly protested, insisting that the human person lives in and with the organic as well as the inorganic. Science is a quest for knowledge and understanding, not just for the useful. It seeks new and creative perspectives; that these bring new categories, biological as well as mathematical, does not mean that all past valuations or theories of knowledge are irrelevant. As a stringent discipline, modern science employs new tools of observation, measurement and calculation. Of course, valuation is more difficult to handle than alleged factual description. Education aims not just at conveying subject matter, but at forming persons capable of sound and responsible judgment. Uncritical belief in science cannot do justice to the subtlety of the issues at stake. The misappropriation of science in a claim for the complete control of human life is no more responsible than religious obscurantism.

Of equal danger with scientism—science becoming the inclusive model for all knowledge—is the isolation of religion from science. More than ever before, a real encounter—open and free—with modern scientific research ought to engage persons interested in religion. Dr. William Pollard, Director of the Oak Ridge Nuclear Laboratory, has been articulate in the attempt to build understanding between science and religion.[5] He points out that modern science is interpretative as well as factual; it has its own community traditions as well as authority, namely, the judgment of experts. Not timeless or simply universal, it has a particular historical orientation in abstraction from one kind of experience. It has its own kind of symbols as well as the inevitable requirement of integrity on the part of those who work in it. Pollard holds that scientific interpretation need not be simply mechanistic or deterministic, indeed it cannot be so, or claim to answer all mysteries. It does not give grounds for regarding the world as self-governing, without special Providence, as was supposed in the Deism of the eighteenth century. Now, there are more dynamic views in both science and religion. Reconciliation or at least cooperation must be based on knowledge of differences in method as well as content between science and religion. Neither can replace the other; recognition of this fact requires that both be given their legitimate place in education.

NOTES

1. Theodor Litt, *Naturwissenschaft und Menschbildung* (Heidelberg: Quelle & Meyer, 1959).
2. Bell, *op. cit.,* p. 121.
3. Karl Jaspers, *Wahrheit und Wissenschaft* (Basel: Helbing & Lichtenhahn, 1960), pp. 12, 21.
4. Alfred North Whitehead, *The Aims of Education* (New York: Mentor, 1949).
5. William G. Pollard, *Chance and Providence: God's Action in a World Governed by Scientific Law* (New York: Scribner, 1958). *Physicist and Christian: A Dialogue Between the Communities* (London: SPCK, 1962).

17

Communism and Religious Education

The accomplishments of Russian education, in which religion is treated negatively, cannot be ignored in discussion of possible philosophies of education as well as church-state relations. Comment evoked by the Communist achievement, especially in scientific training, has dulled appraisal of other factors. Differences in national temperaments and traditions are not to be disregarded. Yet basic disagreements concerning the goals and meaning of education continue to divide East and West. It is interesting to note how often Western educators, visiting the U.S.S.R., are forced to explain their own judgment of the importance of the individual in terms of the Hebrew-Christian tradition. In fact, no other answer is as comprehensive in our cultural legacy. Nor is the issue simply theoretical. It is too often supposed that a valid philosophy or moral interpretation will deliver one from difficult historical problems of competition. In fact, the issues are not so easily resolved. Ideological differences are not necessarily diminished by the mutual desire for peaceful coexistence. Differences in conviction cannot be overcome by appeals to freedom or circumscribed by Western economic power, because they are moral and religious.

They have their basis in inclusive faith premises about what man is and ought to be. The counterpart to Western theism with its doctrine of evil and redemption is the secular utopia of Marx's view of history.

Communism is in fact a many-sided phenomenon, too easily misrepresented in an oversimplified analysis. Marxism is together a social system, political ideology and a faith which makes morality like political theory into a class weapon. Its clear intent is the negation of Christian value judgments. Man's destiny is put exclusively in his own hands; it is not given to him from any transcendent being. Espousing complete freedom from tradition and authority of conscience, Marxism is not practically skeptical or nihilistic. Instead, it demands discipline—the discipline of the Party. Communism as dogmatic allows no middle way; it demands total obedience and control. Yet it would be a mistake to suppose that it does not have intellectual appeal. Indeed, it claims to describe the world in the most reasonable way.

In Marxism, we confront secularism as well as scientism in their naïve dogmatic form.[1] We are to dispense with all mysterious or indescribable unknown. Marxist materialism makes it possible for everything to be understood in principle! The Christian convictions about right and wrong as well as immortality are fantasies of the imagination. Conscience is only the result of training. Change the individual's economic situation and his beliefs too will change. In principle, there is no real distinction between religion and superstition. Communism gives primacy to the whole; the individual exists only for the group. Its paradoxical mixture of a call to action and determinism raises acutely the question of the meaning of human responsibility. Are the difficulties which man experiences primarily economic as Marx holds, or moral as Christianity teaches?

Communism makes all life political. The ideological state is not just an instrument for the unity and harmony of the community; it is the community. Marxism regards the individual less as reason or will than as a place of power. He is the bearer of class interests. There is no universal good valid for all persons. Ideas are the expression of material and social needs and conditions. Justice like ideology exists for class interest. This political view of truth makes the other person an object and seeks to influence him, rather than allowing him to understand what is at stake. In this relativistic outlook, the Party alone is a dependable center of reference. Its will, embodied in history, is the objective and controlling truth. Objectivity is not the antithesis of a private inner life of subjectivity; the latter is considered unimportant. Objectivity belongs only to the Party as it stands over against the selfish class interests of its enemies.

Revolutions such as that which took place in Russia under Communist leadership inevitably bring drastic changes in educational practice. Its initiators almost at once attempted to develop school structures to support their conviction, at first with an unrealistic, utopian view of the possibilities of cultural change. Lenin wrote that during the dictatorship of the proletariat the Party has responsibility to transform the schools into "an instrument for the Communist regeneration of society." [2] Tsarist educational reform, although imposed by despotism, had nevertheless been inspired by Western European Enlightenment ideas. During the nineteenth century, the novelist and philosopher Leo Tolstoi developed a pedagogical theory which was more indigenously Russian.[3] His ideas were creative enough to continue to be influential even into the early Communist era. Like the Marxists, he rejected the dominant political and religious traditions; by contrast to their dialectical materialism, he emphasized natural development and individual freedom. In the end, the new Russian pedagogy came to be formulated in deliberate antithesis to his religious sentiment and concern for the individual. Inevitably, it takes its decisive orientation from the legacy of radical political leadership which had been driven to revolution against a despotism which joined church and state.

The Russian revolution was an awakening to the possibilities of education. Joined with Marx's scientism and dogmatic belief that there is nothing beyond the world of space-time, was an apocalyptic vision of great power. When he wrote, the principle of universal public education was not yet fully established in Western Europe. Education was all too often dominated by privilege and class. Marx did not envisage amelioration under the sponsorship of existing regimes, but revolutionary change. He had a sense of urgency as to how much the world can be reshaped. Part of his legacy to modern Communism is the belief in the radical self-formation of man. This heritage has appeared in Soviet education ever since the time of Lenin. It is characteristically dogmatic, optimistic and self-confident, even in its unprecedented centralization of power. Pluralism is denied. Marx like his successors believed that he had the knowledge and power to remake men and society.

Communism no more than capitalism seems ready to wither away in education. The fact is that the Russian school system has adapted itself to diverse problems and shown significant power of self-reform. Dr. Lawrence Derthick, United States Commissioner of Education, wrote in the period of Sputnik:

We were simply not prepared for the degree to which the U.S.S.R. as a nation is committed to education as a means of national advancement. . . . Our major reaction therefore is one of astonishment—and I choose the word advisedly—at the extent to which it seems to have been accomplished.[4]

Most disturbing was not the military potential offered by Russian technology; it was the fact that the United States had had the resources for such accomplishment before the

Russians and had made no similar attempt. How much present achievement is due to Communism alone, how much to nationalism and the momentum of new technology remains an open question. The positive effect on American thought has been to break down self-complacency and isolation.

Professor George Kline of Columbia University has commented:

> It is doubtful that any society has ever poured such a high proportion of its energies and resources into educational activities, in the broadest sense of the term, as the Soviet Union is doing today. Soviet leaders, from the beginning, have treated organized education with greater seriousness than political leaders in any other country, and this seriousness is widely shared by Soviet students and teachers, at every level of the school system.[5]

Karça concludes that the Soviet educational system has been effective in providing trained personnel for the natural and mathematical sciences.[6] It has developed specialists in the intermediate and higher qualification brackets in the different fields of technology. Less effectiveness has been shown in making adequate adjustment of subject matter to grade levels. Individual abilities and inclinations of students in choice of education or profession have too often been ignored. He writes:

> An important incentive is the fact that under the Soviet regime, where private property has been abolished and no opportunities exist for expressing personal initiative in industry, agriculture, commerce, or other areas of life, the sole condition for a tolerable existence is a diploma from a higher educational institution. To obtain this document, which, together with a Party card, also makes it possible to enter the ruling Communist circles or the ranks of the well-paid intelligentsia, young people in the Soviet Union study with a degree of concentration that is quite unknown in other countries.[7]

Communist education has indeed been remarkably thorough. Its goal is not simply indoctrination, but understanding inspired and liberated by new proletarian ideals. The Soviet attempt to create a new type of man—ready to live and die gladly for the controlled technological society—needs to be appraised realistically. It has too often been supposed that ideology would be modified with new economic growth, a thesis in itself too Marxist! In spite of centralized planning, the Russians have developed a significant dialogue about the problems and structures of education. Their secular ideals have been the basis for a remarkable growth. It is hard to deny that there has been an effective dynamic of change. As late as 1926, 42 percent of the population in European Russia was still illiterate; the percentage was still higher in other regions. By 1939, the figure had been reduced to 19 percent throughout the country. Today, illiteracy appears to be negligible in the U.S.S.R. In 1914, there were 105 institutions of higher education, including eight universities. There were a total of 127,400 students and graduates totaled 10,700. By 1959, 766 institutions of higher learning existed in the U.S.S.R., forty of them universities with 2,150,000 students and 342,200 graduates.[8]

As Nigel Grant points out in his careful and balanced study, *Soviet Education,* a simply negative appraisal of this vast expansion on the grounds that it does not conform to Western democratic patterns would be dangerously naïve.[9] Centralization continues in perpetuation of traditions which date from Tsarist days. Western visitors are generally impressed negatively with the high degree of control in a nationally directed system of education, in spite of Russian claims of local responsibility. The formal character of instruction, use of lecture methods in the lower grades with rote recitation and little discussion or group activity, seems retrogressive over practices followed earlier in the Communist era. Not only textbooks but lesson plans and orders of procedure are planned nationally. At first, the Communists experimented with more individual, less stereotyped practice. The vastness of the educational task to be accomplished as well as the pressure for practical results in science, industry and government led to more rigidly established procedures. Training must end in specific ability, providing leadership for the new technological society. George Counts writes: "No society has ever committed itself so unreservedly in words to the mastery and development of mathematics and natural sciences." [10] Such a development of science has not been free of Party control; indeed, it has an avowedly political goal. Basic decisions of principle and procedure come from Party officials. There is no ambiguity about the intention of maintaining ideological direction.

Especially important is the fact that the Communist Party has parallel structures with government agencies and takes the major role in directing education. Neither parents nor teachers are allowed to interfere in the establishment of policy. Study plans, curricula and textbooks are standardized. The Central Committee of the Communist Party together with the Council of Ministers issues jointly decrees or regulations pertaining to education. Party control is exercised especially through the Komsomol, the older youth organization, and the trade unions. Faculty members and teaching personnel are organized into unions and in turn influence new appointments. Like Komsomol members, they sit on admission committees.

At the Thirteenth Congress of the All-Union Komsomol, Khrushchev initiated discussion of the problems which led to the school reform of December, 1958; the organization has had an important role in the discussion of change. He spoke of the fact that higher education had been available to the children of Communists and elements close to them, more than to children of workers, peasants and petty employees. The latter have been forced to go to work after graduation from secondary schools. This "shameful situation" corrupts "the democratic principles of Soviet Socialism." Young men and women enroll in particular educational institutions not because they desire to work in the field which is taught, but because they wish the prized diploma necessary for status in the society.

We still have a sharp distinction drawn between mental and manual work. . . . This is fundamentally wrong and runs counter to our teaching and aspirations. As a rule, boys and girls who have finished secondary school consider that the only acceptable path in life for them is to continue their education at higher schools. . . . Some of them even consider (work) beneath their dignity. This scornful and lordly attitude is to be found also in some families. If a boy or girl does not study well . . . and fails to get into college, the parents . . . frighten him by saying that if he does not study well and fails to get into college he will have to work in a factory as a common labourer. Physical work becomes a thing to frighten children with. . . . Such views are an insult to the working people of the socialist state.[11]

Particularly deplored was the "incorrect social attitude" of those parents who want to keep their children in white collar jobs in contempt of manual work. It has its counterpart in the working classes who seek an advanced social position for their offspring which will avoid productive labor. Part of revivification is supplied by an increased emphasis on polytechnical training. Earlier, vocationalism was attacked by Communist leaders as a capitalist intrigue for enslaving the working classes. Of course, the new policy was in part its adaptation. Yet it has some basis in the dictum of Marx himself that students should be familiar with the basic principles of production and the tools of the productive process. Lenin supported polytechnical education strongly, although it could not be implemented during his lifetime because of a lack of basic tools of modern farm and industry. He advocated technological literacy in criticism of pre-revolutionary schools which served the needs of only a small part of the population. Rapacz, in an analysis of the present development, points out that other than organizational questions or ideology are involved. There is a practical need to care for the disappointed hopes of vocationally ambitious young people.

The Soviets have insisted on a common school which does not separate students according to ability. Classroom units work together. Students who are more advanced in a given area are expected to help others toward achievement. The common school was restructured in 1958 to provide for an eight-year program. The child comes to school for his first year at the age of seven; he attends classes four hours a day, six days a week. Instruction is given in forty-five minute periods; there are two twenty minute recesses during the day. The subject matter taught includes thirteen hours of Russian, six hours of mathematics, two hours of physical education, one hour each of music, drawing and work study. Such a large portion of time can be given to "Russian language and literature," as the title covers a wide field and is not as limited as it first suggests. Work training begins in the first year with simple lessons in the manipulation of tools and materials, sewing, modelling and paper-cutting. Carpentry with allied skills is introduced in the fourth year and various mechanical skills are added later. Foreign language instruction generally begins in the fourth year, but is now given in some schools as early as the second grade. By the time the children reach their eighth and final year, the school day has been increased by an hour and the curriculum includes five hours of Russian literature and language, six hours of mathematics, three hours of history, two hours of geography, three hours of foreign language, three hours of physics, two hours of chemistry, two hours of biology, three hours of physical education, three hours of labor training and two hours of "socially useful labor."

School training is related to the work of other character-building agencies. The most important of these is the youth movement which operates on large state subsidies. It is organized at three levels: the Octobrists for younger children, the Pioneers for children between the ages of ten and fifteen and the Komsomol for young people between fifteen and twenty-seven. Although membership is voluntary, virtually all children belong to the Young Pioneers. Detachments are organized in every class in school; each detachment is further divided into small informal groups. Initiation at the age of ten is made an especially important occasion. The initiation ceremony takes place in a school, Pioneer Palace or factory and is accompanied by appropriate speeches of exhortation. At the appropriate time in the school year, the teacher together with Pioneers from higher classes explains the importance, duties and privileges of the Pioneer organization to children who are approaching their tenth birthday. The new members accept the rules of the organization and promise: "I, a Young Pioneer of the Soviet Union, in the presence of my comrades solemnly promise to love my Soviet Motherland passionately, and to live, learn and struggle as the great Lenin bade us and as the Communist Party teaches us." They receive a triangular red scarf and badge bearing the motto, "Always Ready." On occasions of severe discipline, the scarf can be taken away from a member as a sign of reprimand. The movement sponsors some 2,500 Pioneer Palaces and Houses where children can go to follow hobbies and interests in their spare time. Some located in rural areas are not too impressive. Others in urban centers are great buildings such as the Pioneer Republic opened in Moscow in June, 1962. Special attention is given to encouragement of interest in nature and to providing opportunities for its study.

By contrast with the Pioneers which include the majority of eligible children, only about a third of the older students enroll in the Komsomol or older youth group. Projects of the Komsomol are diverse and extend into all fields of national life. Discipline is stringent and there are important work assignments. For example, members of the Komsomol help in Pioneer camps, work in harvests on collective farms and construct sites for community projects. Part of the Leningrad subway system was built by Komsomol members. The organization has branches in each faculty of the university, with representatives on every administrative body. A good record as a Komsomol member offers the prospect of a worthwhile position in later life as well as entrance into Communist Party membership.

It is characteristic of the Russian educational system that it is organized carefully under central control. The individual is constantly supervised and his ability and character appraised critically. His past record follows him. In the lower grades, marks are given for discipline. Censorship by the class itself is generally effective in controlling defectors. If not, parents may be called on and social pressure exerted on them as necessary. Competition for admission to the universities is keen. Nearly twice as many hours of classroom study are required at the university level as in the United States, and it is generally agreed that reading lists are excessive. Yet the professional necessity of university training remains for all those who wish advancement. Indoctrination in Communist philosophy is required for all students. Although its acceptance is at times unenthusiastic, there is little revolt in favor of another view, for example, Christianity. Hatred of the capitalist classes, the superiority of the Soviet over the bourgeoisie system, as well as class loyalty rather than concern for all mankind, are commonplace in Communist teaching.

Communist ideology is dogmatic but not nihilistic. Its rejection of the tradition of Western humanism is at the same time a denial of any universal norms for action or any intrinsic knowledge. Practically, it disavows the possibility of maintaining group effort and discipline while still considering the individual as an end in himself. The Communist state assuredly has had unprecedented power of centralization reinforced by technology. The new order for which it works is described as "scientific." Science, with the consequent economic change which it has effected, makes man free. It enables man to deal with his own self. The state and economy are organized together. Without doubt, Communism has been more effective in education than the old Tsarist regime.

Schlette argues convincingly that it is of basic importance to understand why metaphysics is negated in Marxist dialectical materialism.[12] The new type of Soviet pedagogy disavows any intellectual or moral "realm" beyond empirical experience. Instead, it claims a thoroughly dynamic understanding of nature and community. Communist education seeks to evoke openness to the dialectic of history, rather than concern for static concept. Intellectual perspectives are believed to reflect dominant economic and social conditions. Nature and community, both interpreted as this-worldly, are the poles on which Marxist educational practice is oriented. Neither is to be interpreted subjectively, but from the objectivity of scientific analysis.

Lenin stated clearly that Communist education should not be universal or classless in the Western sense.[13] It is to be basically political, not disinterested, and under the authority of the Party. Communist educational optimism lies in the affirmation that scientific, that is empirical, investigation can unlock all mysteries. Teaching is not oriented on individual freedom or good will, both of which are irrelevant or even destructive when they thwart the dynamics of change. It is the responsibility of the Communist Party to structure society in such a way that it conforms to the dialectic of history. Of course, there can be no real conflict

between the views of the Party and any objective transcendent truth. There is no truth outside or beyond history
bearing intrinsic meanings. There is only process in the
space-time world.

Continuing from Tsarist times is the inheritance of a
unified curriculum with respect to fundamentals. This is
reflected today in the comprehensive school structure. Study
plans are nation-wide with variation only in the type of
specialized training. Attainment of specialization at a definite
level of education brings social mobility. Those who achieve
membership in the new classes put stress on being cultured.
Nonetheless, equalitarianism remains as an ideal. This was
evident in the widespread protest against plans to establish
specialized schools in the 1958 reforms. Equalitarianism has
been fostered by the refusal to admit innate differences.
Formerly, it was held that such handicaps as blindness or
deafness could not be the result of heredity; they came rather
from damage done to the fetus during pregnancy or birth.
Now, there is the continuing claim that differences can be
narrowed by proper manipulation of environment. A child
with slow comprehension, for example, can compensate for
his handicap by extra memory training. In fact, there is
continuing class distinction. Educational opportunities have
not been equal for children of peasants or the lower working
class. At the upper levels, special purpose institutions may
be converted into socially divisive schools with limited enrollment. Yet the motivation for learning is strong. Bereday
quotes the remark cited by a Harvard research study: "In
the Soviet Union people without education are not considered people. They are just like horsepower." [14]

In spite of an atheistic emphasis, major attention is given
to moral training in the Soviet schools. The character development of the child is appraised by special staff members.
Discipline is based on twenty standard "Rules for Pupils."

The student is expected not only to know what they are, but why they have been established. If he violates the standard of the class, he may be called on by his teacher to identify the precept which he has broken. The first begins: "It is the duty of every school child to acquire knowledge persistently in order to become an educated and cultured citizen and to be of the greatest possible service to his country." Although many of the rules are quite detailed, they give a clear picture of what is going on in the schools as well as what is expected. Nothing could be more mistaken than to suppose that Communist practice is amoral, even though it denies any transcendent good. Instead, it insists on the group values which it seeks to inculcate directly; to this end it enlists the cooperation of parents and youth organizations as well as public communication media. Teacher training courses give careful attention to character development. Goals and methods of procedure are precise and detailed. Until the child is eleven, through his fourth year in school, major attention is directed to habit formation. His basic character is to have been established by this time, and there follows a changed emphasis on rational appreciation for the need of particular traits. The objectives of teaching include:

1) Soviet patriotism and a feeling of friendship among peoples.
2) Realization of social duty.
3) Discipline, persistence and endurance, including "distinguishing between caution and cowardice, between boldness and recklessness."
4) Friendship and comradeship, one instance of which is "telling a comrade tactfully the truth to his face and helping him to find the right solution."
5) Attentive and thoughtful attitudes toward people.
6) Truthfulness, honesty and modesty; apart from the avoidance of lying, this is taken to comprise having a "proper attitude" to criticism and being able to resist bad influences such as "rowdyism, profanity, gambling . . . idleness."

7) Responsible attitudes toward study and work, including concern for the study achievements of the whole class.[15]

In principle, any supernatural or metaphysical basis of
moral values is denied. In the Communist view, a moral code
is a device which serves the needs of a particular society at
a given time. It evokes group loyalty and insures cooperation
of citizens. As socially derived, it meets particular needs of
the time and helps the society to run more smoothly. Communist teaching encourages the student to take pride in the
tradition of the Russian Revoluion, the precepts of Lenin
and the rule of the Party. Grant points out that some Communist writers now accept the idea that there are basic values
which operate to the benefit of mankind at large and are
valid for all societies.[16] However, they have no transcendent
moral basis and their utility is derived from social needs
quite apart from any question of belief in God.

Anton Semenovich Makarenko (1888–1939) is not only
acclaimed as the leading Soviet educator; his ideas have a
place of dominance somewhat comparable with that of
Dewey in the United States.[17] By contrast, his outlook is
collectively oriented. Makarenko's presuppositions are genuinely and exclusively those of Marxist political ideology
as distinguished from Western humanism: this-worldly, politically unquestioning and collectivistic. His career as a
teacher was an impressive one. Born in a small railroad
center in the Ukraine, Makarenko received a firm sense of
discipline under parental guidance. His family relationship
was one of mutual effort, obedience and love, traits which
he later advocated for the Soviet family. A short period of
military service left a lasting influence on his pedagogical
outlook, showing itself in a sense of discipline and cama-
raderie. Makarenko was influenced by Socialism ever since
the unrest of 1905. When the new regime was established
under Lenin, he espoused its outlook actively. From 1920 to

1935, he was leader of two school colonies for displaced children, many of whom were war orphans. He named the first colony in honor of his admired literary leader, Gorki; it was located near Poltava and later Kurjaz. The second, the Dzerzinskij near Char'kav, came under his direction in 1928. Makarenko's communities became models for visitors from both Russia and abroad. In recognition of his success, he was promoted to a government office for the Ukraine and transferred to Kiev in 1935. By 1937, he had become a national figure and moved to Moscow. Makarenko's pedagogical writings include poetry, a book of advice for parents as well as other volumes on educational theory and practice in general.

Makarenko's practical educational genius can hardly be denied. His colony took children who had had no care or discipline and developed them into responsible citizens in spite of the most difficult conditions. The economic resources available to the colony were severely limited in the early period after the revolution. Yet it became a productive, earning community with a common life of work and study. Makarenko's appealing personality, contagious devotion and responsible sense of discipline evoked the best from his charges. He often disregarded their past records, casting aside the files of tests and records which had been sent to him. As he was especially perceptive in his judgment of persons, his students responded successfully to his interest in them. In short, his was an individual and practical rather than a consistently structured or "scientific" pedagogical approach oriented on established procedures. His outlook was polytechnic, inasmuch as it joined productive work with study. Active political participation was carried on with moral discipline in the life of the community.

The total life of the colony member, his status, rewards and punishments, was oriented completely on the collective. Such was the self-conscious intention of Makarenko's pedagogy—which he held to be responsible for his success. He believed that the personality of the child takes its rise from and is shaped by the larger social group. The goal of education is one of free assent to the group leadership with the individual being willingly structured from his social relationships. The collective as a living, organic group unites its members through common struggle, work and responsible joint solution to problems. The community gives life a character and a worthwhileness which its members could not achieve by themselves. As head of the colony, Makarenko retained the right of punishment, but exercised it moderately. He conceived of his role as an educator as one of leadership rather than of dominance. The collective was to discipline its own members who in turn were to know why group action was taken against them. The teacher is to encourage all his charges not only by relevant interest in their vocational goals, but responsible moral guidance, acceptance, concern and love.

In a number of important respects, Makarenko's colony had similarities with Father Flanagan's Boys' Town. Yet the final goal of education could hardly have been conceived more differently. Makarenko was unfriendly to any religious feeling or expression on the part of his charges, and criticized openly all claims of belief in God on their part. Rejecting religious ritual, he developed his own "secular" ceremonies which were designed to evoke appropriate feelings of loyalty. They took their model from his military experience: important occasions were celebrated with flags and uniforms. A student was not to value abstract knowledge egoistically but to experience concrete and relevant growth through group relations. Collective life has the self-conscious purpose of producing a new type of man, one free of both otherworldly goals and self-destructive individualism. Personal integration follows as the group is served in patriotism and moral purpose. As genuinely Marxist in ideology, the community shares in the larger class struggle. The spirit of the collective—its demands and promise—is to carry over into family life. The child learns that positive rewards and benefits come from loyalty to the Communist cause. Makarenko's advice to parents is oriented on group responsibility rather than individualism. The child is not to be trained as an aristocrat who disavows manual labor, but as a willing member of the working class.

As Froese points out, the defects of such pedagogy are not difficult to identify.[18] The concern for class and nation takes dominance over any more universal humanism. Patriotism is primary: Russia is the great homeland which can nurture Socialism and spread the new way of life. Freedom is not a pretext for selfishness or moral confusion as among the bourgeois. The party has a kind of "pastoral role" in supplying basic values. Denied is any abiding pluralism or individualism; the person takes his sanctions from the group. No transcendent moral norms or religious truth are to be recognized. Instead, the pupil is to see himself as caught up in a this-worldly struggle of the working class, which is dramatized for him even in his own collective. The group is what matters and not personal advancement. Nature and reason are not argued about; theory develops from, and with practice in, a characteristic Marxist way.

Marx, of course, held that religion is an opium of the people which lulls the working class. Lenin described it as a kind of "spiritual moonshine, by which the slaves of capitalism lose their human personality, their aspirations for something more dignified as human beings." [19] During the Second World War there was a limited truce in the attacks on organized religion. Since the end of the war, there has been an overt renewal of the anti-religious campaign. Floridi cites an article in an educational publication devoted to methods of teaching in the secondary schools:

The youngsters must be taught that: (a) religion always depends on material circumstances and does not respond to a deep and lasting need in man; (b) religion and the church, especially the Roman Catholic Church, are always reactionary, and that religious morality and Communist morality are always fundamentally antagonistic to one another; (c) religion and science are irreconcilable; and finally, (d) the students must know the Party policies toward religion. Objective descriptions of and comparative differences between creeds must be avoided in teaching, since this could produce the contrary effect, that is, it could propagate religion. To find out which pupils come from religious families, the teacher will ask: "Who will tell me something about the origins of religion?" The teacher will then require the pupils to transcribe the most important quotations of anti-religious authors, such as Engels, for example, "Every religion is nothing but a reflection in the fancy of men of the external forces that dominate them in daily life." [20]

Soviet education is required to be positively atheistic. It has been found that where non-religious teaching is allowed without overt attack, religion persisted. The teacher is to insist on the scientific deduction which the majority of students generally do not make. For example, after having explained the Newtonian law of universal gravitation in physics instruction, he is to add that before the discovery of this law man attributed to God a "supernatural force" which explains the orderly movement of the celestial bodies. Of course, the teacher is not to report to the students that Newton remained a theist!

A larger concern is given to the positive teaching of history than to negative anti-religious emphasis. Russian teaching of history abounds with a sense of Communist world mission. Factual narration is adapted to the view that Communism will bring salvation in the final solution of man's problems. History is taught by itself rather than mixed with other social studies. The teaching of historical concepts begins in the second and third grades. By the fifth and sixth grades at age twelve and thirteen, pupils are regarded as able to understand the most complicated generalizations on the historical process if the data are presented clearly and discussed correctly. All of the humanities are taught under the limits of Marxist presuppositions and perspectives, in the spirit of mid-nineteenth century dogmatic rationalism and naturalism.

A variety of historical figures including Radishev, Push-kin, Lermontov, Nekrasov, Saltykow-Shchedrin, Mendeleyev and Tolstoy are described as precursors of present-day militant atheism.[21] Lomonosov, the alleged founder of Moscow University, is described similarly. Actually, the University was initiated by Count I. I. Shuvalov who employed Lomonosov to work out plans for curriculum and organization. Lomonosov was a kind of Renaissance man who combined great talent for poetry and philosophy with important discoveries in electricity, meteorology, optics, astronomy and geology. At the celebration of the bi-centennial of Moscow University in 1955, he was hailed by Russian newspapers as "the father of materialistic-philosophical thought in Russia." In fact, he wrote *Spiritual Odes,* a free translation of the Psalms and other parts of the Old Testament. Together with his *Reflections on the Greatness of God,* they were adapted by the Russian Old Believers in their liturgy. It is characteristic of Communist anti-religious propaganda that it works on the marginal aspects of religion, such as superstition, fables, prejudices, and ridicules feasts, rites, miracles and prophecies. Khrushchev once acknowledged that it is often based on anecdotes and fables. There are a variety of films for school use, all attacking religion in the name of science. Lenin wrote:

We must not, in any event, err by putting the religious question on an abstract and idealistic basis, in rational terms, re-

moved from the class war, as the democratic radical bourgeoisie so often does.[22]

If Communism has been effective in producing an exclusively secular context of education, what is to be the
Western democratic strategy in competition? There is no
reason to minimize the extent of the Soviet achievement in
education. Its accomplishment in rebuilding has been very
great, following the Second World War. No doubt, patriotic
national feeling has supported and increased the power of
public education. Nigel Grant has called attention to some
of the intrinsically positive features of the Soviet system.
He believes that a variety of aspects of its youth movement
could well be copied in the West. Without doubt, there
has been a serious concern for public morals in control of
mass media entertainment available to younger age groups.
Of course, some state strategies are in part a substitute for
religious sanctions. It is tragic that positive accomplishment
has been accompanied by dogmatic anti-religious propaganda, in part as a revolt against a legacy of abuse in the
past. A more adequate educational program would not necessarily require renewed church control, but only a willingness to treat religion more fairly.

In the end, Communism appeals to the dynamics of history
and personal life, in a way that high religion alone can
answer. More important than any anti-Communist ideology
or propaganda in the West, is responsible understanding of
one's own cultural background and presuppositions. Is public education to present real options, social, political and
religious, or is it to perpetuate the indolence of conformity?
What better way can there be to serve Communist ends than
to bar the religious critique which alone can deal with the
full dimensions of the problem. The issues are not simply
sectarian or confessional. It is important that Americans
begin to see and understand what Marxism is saying in rela-

tion to their religious heritage—not at the level of politics but of education. Until they do so, they will not have come to a maximum effort in the face of totalitarian competition with Russia or other Communist countries.

NOTES

1. Heinz Robert Schlette, *Sowjethumanismus, Prämissen und Maximen kommunisticher Pädagogik* (Munich: Kosel, 1960).
2. George Z. F. Bereday and Jaan Pennar, eds., *The Politics of Soviet Education* (New York: Praeger, 1960), p. 4.
3. Leonard Froese, *Ideen geschichtliche Triebkräft Russische und Sowjetische Pädagogik* (Heidelberg: Quelle & Meyer, 1963), pp. 87–144.
4. Nigel Grant, *Soviet Education* (Middlesex, England: Penguin, 1964), p. 162.
5. *Ibid.*
6. Ramazan Karça, "A General View of Soviet Education," *The Politics of Soviet Education, op. cit.,* pp. 4–27.
7. *Ibid.,* p. 5.
8. Grant, *op. cit.,* p. 108.
9. *Ibid.,* p. 151.
10. *Ibid.,* pp. 101–102.
11. Richard V. Rapacz, "Polytechnical Education and the New Soviet School Reforms," *The Politics of Soviet Education,* pp. 28–44.
12. Schlette, *op. cit.,* pp. 19f.
13. Jaan Pennar, "Party Control over Soviet Schools," *The Politics of Soviet Education,* pp. 45–56.
14. George Z. F. Bereday, "Class Tensions in Soviet Education," *The Politics of Soviet Education,* pp. 57–88.
15. Grant, *op. cit.,* pp. 48–49.
16. *Ibid.,* p. 50.
17. Froese, *op. cit.,* pp. 216–281.
18. *Ibid.*
19. Alessio U. Floridi, "Antireligious Education of Soviet Youth," *The Politics of Soviet Education,* pp. 89–99. V. I. Lenin, *Sochineniya,* 4th ed. (Moscow, 1952), X, p. 66.
20. Floridi, *op. cit.,* p. 90.
21. *Ibid.,* p. 94.
22. *Ibid.,* p. 95.

18

Prospects and Conclusions

The revolutionary impact of popular education as it has developed throughout the nineteenth and twentieth centuries can hardly be overstated. The educational revolution continues today with the spread of literacy in the under-developed countries. It is imperative that church and synagogue should support and contribute to the liberation which this brings. Persons interested in religion ought not to expect full agreement about the ends of education in a democratic society. Indispensable, however, are openness and communication. This is as true in the area of religion as any other. As Arthur Cohen points out, the American Constitution followed a careful middle course: it did not attempt to establish religion, on the one hand, or to invoke measures limiting cult or practice on the other.[1] He emphasizes that it is especially important that belief in freedom itself should not take the place of religion. Cohen's comments are included in a discerning pamphlet, *Religion and the Free Society,* published by the Fund for the Republic. We shall cite some of its conclusions which reflect a growing consensus among spokesmen of different confessional views.

William Miller, writing in the same study, points out that the subordination of the traditional religions to a superior civic faith takes its own particular form in a democracy. Religion is regarded as "divisive." [2] Of course, one may have his own religious belief if he wishes, but no authentic truth claim is allowed. In such circumstances, public school practice all too easily excludes any real theological concern as dangerous to democracy. Such policy is not neutral, but carries its own secular faith claims.

Also writing under the auspices of the Fund for the Republic, William Clancy remarks that the word of Justice Douglas that Americans are a "religious people" could have been better phrased: we are a "reverential" people. Fortunately, we have escaped the dogmatic anti-religion that has infected other societies. However, religion is made part of our public life largely as a matter of fellowship and good works. "Rather than providing a basis for unity in our society, therefore, efforts to introduce any specific, dogmatically grounded religion into public life usually lead to frustration and ill-will." [4] There is widespread distrust of particular theological dogmas and most of all of ecclesiastical authority. As Miller points out, the ethos of public education inevitably reflects the convictions of the whole society.[5] Too often, freedom of religion has been interpreted to mean than one man's ideas are equally as good as those of any other. Of course, in such circumstances the criticism and creativity which Judaism and Christianity have brought to bear on culture in the past are necessarily silenced.

Miller protests rightly against the relativism and anti-intellectualism which allow no abiding religious meaning. They are especially dangerous in education as the integrity of the mind is sacrificed. Too often, education has been regarded simply pragmatically as initiation into community mores and practice.[6] The fact remains that such initiation could be accomplished more cheaply and easily by other

means. We have stressed, rather, that education is an introduction into a whole intellectual tradition based on the
premise of freedom and responsibility. It is only as teaching
is concerned for the growth of individuals—intellectual or
moral—that the question of value emerges. Of course, the
line between a voluntarism which respects freedom of opinion and a relativism which in effect derogates truth is not
an easy one to draw. Dogmatic secularism, often masked
under the title of freedom, simply is not adequate to the
complexity of present moral issues. The real problem is not
how to keep religion out of education; rather, how shall
it be given a responsible place in which it can make its contribution to community life in a pluralistic society. Fortunately, there is a growing recognition that scientific discovery no more than new educational methods can resolve
basic value conflicts. As Dawson remarks, technological success may direct attention away from them: every great civilization has had its basis in some kind of religious commitment which transcends it.[7] Dawson argues further that it is
illusory to suppose that Western society can maintain power
or integrity when its own faith bases are confused or even
derogated.

Mark DeWolfe Howe of the Harvard Law School has
stated convincingly that the restrictions of the First Amendment were not intended initially as a statement of educational policy.[8] They were meant simply as a limitation on
the power of the national government, guarding against
establishment of any church or churches. The Amendment's
scope is extended far beyond its original purpose when it is
interpreted as requiring uniformity in teaching, or even the
exclusion of religion. In fact, at the time of its enactment,
education was largely the responsibility of religious groups.
The Amendment's historical context was one of federalism.
The polity which it initiated stands in strong contrast to the
centralized control of public education in continental Eu-

rope which grew up with the French Revolution, German imperialism and Russian Communism.[9] Instead, school organization in the United States followed the English model of decentralization. The national government did not expect to dominate community life, much less control all of culture. Its powers were limited in principle by the Constitution whose provisions were intended to protect the autonomy of business, educational and religious life.

Arthur Cohen emphasizes that the Constitution prescribes, as a fundamental principle, that the claims of government as well as of religious institutions should be regarded as self-limiting.[10] Although faith makes an absolute claim at the religious level, this consideration ought not to be used to extend the prerogatives of the religious group indefinitely throughout public life. The success of disestablishment depends not alone on state policy, but on community attitudes as well. The Founding Fathers were clear that they wished to avoid the privileges of establishment. Regarding religious groups as fallible and subject to error, they developed a policy in which the different denominations would be circumscribed by checks and balances of the common life. Separation of church and state did not mean the exclusion of religion; instead, it was to penetrate culture but not by coercion. Voluntarism did not require a socially irresponsible individualism. Instead, church and synagogue have a responsible place in public life, influencing society openly.

Seeking clear definition of the problem of separation of church and state, Clancy argues that the metaphor of "the wall" is inexact and confusing. The United States has been uniquely fortunate for a tradition which recognizes a distinction between two orders of competence.

"The wall" of separation between Church and State, as it is conceived by most "absolute separationists" in America, is not really a constitutional concept. It is rather a private doctrine (of a militant secularism in some cases, of one version of Christian theology in others) which a minority of Americans seem intent on imposing on all. Many of the battles that now rage over "Church-State" issues tell more about the growth of dogmatic secularism in our society than they do about the Constitution.[11]

Clancy adds, emphasizing his conviction: "To the extent that the 'absolute wall' theory is supported in the courts, to that same extent a doctrine about which the Constitution itself knows nothing has been imposed on American life." [12]

Among the authors of the pamphlet published by the Fund for the Republic, there is not full agreement but a growing consensus. For example, there is recognition that the exclusion of all specifically credal aspects of religion can come only at the cost of a thinly veiled secular dogmatism. It is the silencing of religious options which is in fact really sectarian. Of course, such restraint is difficult to avoid if religious groups are concerned only with what is distinctive about their own respective points of view. Professor Wilbur G. Katz of the University of Wisconsin spoke about this problem in his Rosenthal Lectures at the Northwestern University School of Law:

The fear of "divisiveness," I take it, is a fear that, if religious differences are publicly recognized, the result is to accentuate the divisions and to exacerbate hostilities already existing. This danger is not imaginary and under some social conditions it may be a controlling consideration. . . .

But when we are discussing constitutional policy, the question is different. Are we to interpret the First Amendment on the assumption that serious hostility is the norm in interfaith relations and that legislatures and school boards should therefore be enjoined to take note of religion only by staying away from it? [13]

Katz cites with approval the position of Vialatoux and Latreille, two French laymen who are professors in French universities, as understanding the proper secular character of the State.

This ideal laicity can be called neutrality inasmuch as it denies itself the decision concerning the form which the act of religious liberty will take. . . . But it is not the neutrality of someone who is unaware of religion or who scorns it.[14]

Our concern has not been primarily with parochial institutions or the degree of state support which should be given to their activities. It has been rather for a legitimate place for teaching about religion in public education. As the American Council on Education report emphasizes, it is imperative that this latter interest should be distinguished from control of education by religious bodies.[15] Only as long as it is recognized that public education cannot be surrendered to confessional dominance, whatever may be the majority religious opinion in the community, can we expect teaching about rather than teaching for religion. Religionists who wish to capture the public school system for their own sectarian ends can be resisted on clear constitutional grounds. This is not to say that organized religion ought not to have a voice in public school efforts to give religion the relevance it deserves in the spirit of freedom. Church and synagogue are after all the chief centers of religious interests in the community. It is imperative that leaders as well as their constituencies understand that concern for religion in public education can be effective only as it reflects the widest possible interest and not sectarian pressure.

The danger of a vacuum, when religionists retreat behind confessional barriers, is altogether too evident. Clancy writes: "With the emergence of an increasingly technological, depersonalized and secularized culture, it is clearly the role of religion to stand more strongly than ever as a witness to the spiritual and transcendent aspects of life."[16] Realistically, he points out the danger of a growing alienation between religion and secular culture in a pluralistic society. Religion seems to reject the secular culture as rebellion, and secular culture in turn tends to excommunicate spokesmen for religion as a force of an anachronistic authoritarianism. Part of the resolution of the dilemma is to be found in a clear understanding of terms: in the distinction between "secular" and "secularism." Cohen is assuredly correct in pointing out that the secular may be viewed in two different ways.[17] In its original meaning, it was the non-holy, that portion of the human order which had not yet been penetrated by religious values. Our problem is that in the course of time it has acquired another meaning, namely, an order of society which is neutral to the influence of religion. The secular has been converted into secularism, making it the de facto opponent of religion. In public education, especially, careful distinction must be made between these two interpretations. The Constitution is not characterized by the second meaning: it allows religion free entry into the secular order but without political support!

Every religious group would like to have its conviction established fully in the society. The plain fact is that under an all-or-nothing approach, absolutism has led to a situation in which religion is being excluded from public education. For a time, specifically theological teaching was replaced in the common school by moral philosophy. Now, the challenge to religious conviction has become more overt. Many religious groups may not be ready for teaching about religion. If their view is to prevail, there can remain only a no man's land between education and religion. Of course, what is needed is not an ecclesiastical consensus imposed on education; it could have little positive effect. Most important is a climate of opinion in which problems and issues can be explored openly by school and community leaders. Under such circumstances, structures can be adjusted within legal limits to meet common concerns of principle.

The Supreme Court has ruled that the Constitution intends the disestablishment of all religions. One can ask legitimately whether what the Court meant is clearly understood. It did not necessarily intend to set up an essentially defensive situation in which teachers and administrators avoid religious issues. The very rights the Court enjoins for freedom of conscience become meaningless without some larger affirmation of abiding values. The fact is that most Americans are not prepared to accept a simply relativistic doctrine of truth. There is a significant consensus, more perhaps than the Supreme Court has recognized. The basic issue of public policy is how to guard and extend this consensus, not how to reduce it to ineffectiveness. The state makes demands for responsible conduct, justice and tolerance. Should it not also encourage the community forces which will strengthen motivation toward these ends? The issue is not simply one of authority or the institutional role of religion. It is one of the ethos of the society itself.

Jefferson opposed Protestant denominational interference in public education because it prejudiced an understanding of the common religious heritage.[18] His rejection of establishment was not intended to signalize the absence of religious ideas in teaching, but to encourage their discussion in a context which transcends that of any single Protestant group. Religious faith, expressed freely, was to give integrity and renewal to civic life. In the end, Jefferson's hope that denominationalism would diminish proved mistaken. Sectarian hostility became the initiating factor in secularization. Now, nineteenth-century patterns of piety and community organization remain, but they are no longer dominant. Increased urbanization, new technology as well as changed international conditions have brought different dimensions to group life. The problem of religious education is more complex than in earlier rural America, not only because of the growth of mass media of information, but in view of new intellectual concerns.

At present, a whole variety of new information as well as interpretation in many different fields is bringing about an explosion of knowledge. Is public education to appraise this new understanding on exclusively non-religious grounds because of a state policy of secularism? No doubt, admission of the legitimacy of religious concerns in education raises a particular set of administrative problems. To secularize the classroom without qualification, exaggerating differences between religious groups, is a negative and not a positive strategy. Secularism as a thoroughgoing state policy means that the theism, to which the majority of the American people are committed, cannot really become a position in public education. Actually, religion is not necessarily excluded from education by the First Amendment; the Supreme Court has recognized this fact. Sectarian pleading has often made it irrelevant—but it remains indigenous to teaching and learning.

Too often, Protestants have vacillated between a position which makes such minimum demands on belief and conduct as to have little relevance for education and a literalism which a responsible educator must disavow. Much of the earlier Protestant sectarian controversy must be explained from a lack of understanding of the historical background of Biblical religion. Now, Protestant, Roman Catholic and Jewish scholars have come to a larger agreement about the growth of ideas in the Bible record; in short, it is not as much as before a source of sectarian controversy. There are now forces within Protestantism as well as Roman Catholicism and Judaism which look for a vital encounter with contemporary needs and problems. They recognize that the Biblical view of life is not simply one of individual piety, but carries major social concern in its demand for justice. Serious religious leadership, Protestant, Roman Catholic and

Jewish, asks how it is possible to convey Biblical insights in so profound a way that they carry with them the possibility of renewal. To say the least, this is not possible if there is not a working knowledge of the Hebrew-Christian tradition itself in education.

Parents and teachers recognize an abiding threat of nihilism which in the end can make democracy meaningless. Irresponsible behavior and simple hedonism as well as antisocial action—robbery and murder—are continually portrayed by mass media; even before the child can develop resistance against them, he sees them as commonplace. Negative attitudes range all the way from materialism and sensuality to an exhausted intellectualism which has lost all faith that life has any real meaning. What can freedom or justice signify in such an "empty" world? Suppose that they can be justified on utilitarian premises—but for what purpose? Our question is whether a mature civilization can be really motivated by such agnosticism. Culture is an achievement of human creativity and intelligence. Science or business alone do not supply adequate models for it. Apart from religion, education all too easily produces technically clever people who can make money or bombs, but have nothing to live for. The fact that the majority of Americans continue to share a positive attitude toward religion cannot be ignored in education. It is in this context that the common religious heritage of Jews, Roman Catholics and Protestants deserves larger attention than it has received from either the courts or the churches.

Does pluralism mean that religious witness must be completely personal?[19] If so, the traditions of American life will have undergone basic reorientation. To be sure, the older unity of religion and culture by which men have lived in the past has been called in question in both Europe and the United States. A new synthesis is hardly possible apart from the recognition that Western man's major cultural goals and

ethical insights have been derived from faith commitments.
The Hebrew-Christian tradition finds ultimate value beyond
civilization in a higher Being who judges and redeems human life. On this premise, it rejects all cultural absolutism.
Prophetic religion no more than democracy looks for a
closed society. It is not bound to the traditions of the past
without relevance to the present. Yet relevance does not
imply relativism about truth. The dynamic factor of the
Hebrew-Christian tradition is life before God. High religion
contributes to the common life in the most significant way,
by engendering a sense of righteousness and personal responsibility.

Apologists for progressive education have pointed out that
goals and values of the past become irrelevant in changed
conditions. Certainly, but what sort of re-evaluation is to be
looked for? Is "scientific method" to take the place of philosophy and religion? The pattern of change is not as simple
as the progressivists in education have suggested. Too often,
modern man is separated from the past and alienated from
any abiding sense of value and personal meaning. The
utopian view that change is inevitably good easily turns to
nihilism. Existentialism more than pragmatism has attempted
to grapple with the meaninglessness which has appeared in
Western society in the era of the two world wars. It has
recognized that life values cannot be established simply from
what works. The question remains whether it can give any
abiding norms apart from religion. To be sure, existentialism
has taken theistic as well as non-theistic forms.

The Hebrew-Christian conviction is that God and not
religion is ultimate. It is on this premise that differences are
finally to be appraised for the religiously oriented person.
The major Western religions are not a static whole, simply
sectarian or intolerantly dogmatic, but are deeply sensitive
to changing circumstances. Increasingly, disagreements
among believers are being faced in objective, open discus-

sion and not passed over in silence. We have argued that the real crisis of the time is one of values: what can make life worth living in an era set amid the tragedy of two world wars? Evil is a continuing fact of history. It is not self-evident, as is so often presupposed, that man can make and control his own destiny. Democracy allows freedom for personal re-evaluation, but does not itself supply unity of meaning. Is the alternative really a state church with imposition of religion or a radically secular public life? Granted that conscience cannot be compelled, does tolerance require complete neutrality with respect to values and an abiding ground of meaning?

Following the Supreme Court decisions on prayer and Bible reading, a commission of the American Association of School Administrators undertook a careful re-evaluation of the place of religion in public education. Its well considered statement puts the continuing problem clearly:

A curriculum which ignored religion would itself have serious religious implications. It would seem to proclaim that religion has not been as real in men's lives as health or politics or economics. . . . Whatever else the Supreme Court decisions may or may not have done, they have stimulated the public schools to a search for appropriate means to deal effectively with religion as one of the great influences in man's history. . . .

The task is challenging. No perfect answers have been found. But the Commission believes that better and more appropriate materials and methods will be developed as the nature of the challenge is more widely understood, and as educators themselves move to meet it. The answers are not to be expected from those who either do not understand or do not accept the distinction between teaching *about* religion and teaching *for* religion, between examining religion as a cultural phenomenon and indoctrinating in a religion. Neither will they come from those who, misreading the requirement of neutralism, eliminate all references to religion or seem to substitute a non-theistic human-

ism. The constructive contributions will be made by those who
are sensitive to the delicacy and intricacy of the task; who can
combine the contributions of the wisest students of the humanities with those of the most knowledgeable students of teaching
and learning; who can call upon the ablest public school teachers, and who have the courage and resources to provide for
continuous objective evaluation and appropriate revision. This
is a big order, but one infinitely worth the effort.[20]

NOTES

1. *Religion and the Free Society* (New York: The Fund for the Republic,
   1958): Arthur Cohen, "The Problem of Pluralism," p. 35.
2. *Ibid.*, "Religion and the American Way of Life," p. 13.
3. *Ibid.*, "Religion as a Source of Tension," p. 25.
4. Clancy, p. 26.
5. Miller, p. 20.
6. Miller, p. 15.
7. Dawson, *The Crisis of Western Education.*
8. *Religion and the Free Society*, "The Constitutional Question," p. 49.
9. Dawson, *op. cit.*
10. Cohen, p. 38.
11. Clancy, p. 28.
12. Clancy, p. 29.
13. Wilbur G. Katz, *Religion and American Constitutions* (Evanston, Ill.:
    Northwestern University Press, 1964), pp. 55–56.
14. *Ibid.*, p. 22.
15. ACE Studies, XI, No. 26.
16. Clancy, p. 32.
17. Cohen, p. 37.
18. *Cf.* Healey, *op. cit.*
19. Henry J. Van Dusen, *God in Education* (New York: Scribner, 1951).
    Van Dusen's statement on the Regents' Prayer Decision appeared in
    Christianity and Crisis, October 15, 1962.
20. American Association of School Administrators, *Religion in the Public
    Schools* (Washington, D.C., 1964), pp. 55–56.

Index

Adams, John, 37
Africa, 105, 108
Amendments to the U.S. Constitution: First, 3, 10, 26, 36, 230; Fourteenth, 3
American Association of School Administrators, 238
American Civil Liberties Union, 158
American Council on Education, 49, 52, 154, 232
Amery, Carl, 108
Anabaptists, 97
Anglican Church, 127
Antisemitism, 135
Aquinas, Thomas, 87, 156
Asia, 105, 108
Augustine, 85, 106, 156

Baltimore Declaration of Bishops (Third Plenary Council), 17, 145
Baptists, 127
Barth, Karl, 168
Bea, Augustin Cardinal, 109
Beethoven, Ludwig von, 62
Bell, Bernard Iddings, 91, 166, 193, 199
Bennett, John, 193
Bereday, George Z. F., 218
Bergson, Henri, 165
Bible Reading, 4
Biblical Scholarship, 101, 189; Studies, 105
Black, Justice Hugo L., 8, 12, 25
Blanshard, Paul, 32

Blau, Joseph, 178
Bollnow, Otto Friedrich, 74
Brameld, Theodore, 58
Buber, Martin, 182
Buddhism, 56, 162, 164, 167-171

Callahan, Daniel, 146
Calvinists, 97
Cambridge Medieval History, 85
Carr, Peter, 37
China, 167, 169
Christian Civilization, 84; Culture, 81
Church-State Relations, 85, 136, 188, 190; England, 96
Civil War, religion in public schools before, 10
Clancy, William, 229, 231-233
Clark, Justice Tom, 123
Clement of Alexandria, 83-84
Cochrane, Charles Norris, 86
Cohen, Arthur, 29, 35, 228, 231, 234
Cohen, Hermann, 181
Cohen, Seymour J., 178
College Academic Facilities Act of 1963, 148
Colleges, see Higher Education
Common School, 45; in East Germany, 68
Commonweal, 7, 141-146
Communalism, 19, 21, 183
Communism, 168, 206-227; conscience held result of training, 207; hostility to religion, 207, 224; party, role of, 208; science, claims about, 217

241

Comparative Education, 71
Competition, among world religions, 167, 173, 190
Comte, Auguste, 72-73
Conant, James B., 42, 44
Conciliar Movement, 88, 111
Concordat, Germany, 135
Confessional School, 69
Confucius, 167, 170-171
Congar, Yves, 111
Constantine I, Emperor, 84, 121, 180
Constitution, U.S., rights of all citizens, 178
Cremin, Lawrence A., 43, 44
Crime, 117
Cromwell, Oliver, 97

Dawson, Christopher, 49, 59, 78, 81, 82, 88, 164, 230
Decentralization of American school organization, 231
Dechristianization, 109, 131
Deism, 22, 205
Derthick, Lawrence, 209
Desmond, Charles, 6
Determinism, 197, 202, 207
Dewey, John, 12, 44, 57, 59, 220
Dilthey, Wilhelm, 70
Disestablishment, 12, 101, 119
Douglas, Justice William O., 9, 14, 28, 29, 192, 229
Drinan, Robert F., 14, 35
Dual Enrollment, see Shared Time
Dunn, William Kailer, 10

Eastern Orthodoxy, 106
Ecumenical Movement, 98, 100, 104; common scholarly interests, 109
Ecumenical Relations in U.S., 101
Education, current crisis in, 40, 44; revolution in (past), 42-43, 228; world-wide awakening to importance of, 54
Elementary and Secondary Education Act of 1965, 30-35
Eliade, Mircea, 166, 169
Eliot, T. S., 78
Elite, educational, 48
Encyclicals, papal, 140, 142; *Rappresentanti in terra* (Christian Education of Youth), 142; *Rerum Novarum* (The Condition of the Working Classes), 131
Englightenment, 14, 15, 169; influence on Jewish thought, 177, 181, 190-191

Equalitarianism, 40, 47, 128, 218
"Establishment," 93, 127, 231
Evil, problem of, 79, 90
Evolution, biological, 197
Existentialism, 73, 76, 238
Expansion of knowledge in modern period, 146, 236

Federal Subsidy and Support for Education, 41
Founding Fathers, 19, 22, 36
France, religion in schools, 127-133; new democratic pluralism, 133; subsidy to Church schools, 132; Third Republic, 130
Frankfurter, Justice Felix, 26, 33
Free Churches, 101, 107
Free Exercise of Religion, 19, 26
Freedom, 19, 20, 70, 85, 90, 201, 202
Freedom of Conscience, 19, 97, 157, 235
Freedom of Religion, 148, 150, 229
French Revolution, 129-130
Fries, Heinrich, 112
Froese, Leonard, 223
Fundamentalism, 122
Fund for the Republic, 228-229

Gadamer, Hans-Georg, 75
Gandhi, Mahatma, 172
German Christians, 135
Germany, East, common school, 68
Germany, West, 67-76; religion in the public school, 134-137; confessional division, 69, 134; criticism and value of practice, 134; "culture Christianity," Protestant criticism of, 136; Roman Catholic emphasis on daily living, 137
Gierke, Otto von, 87
Gilbert, Arthur, 176
Gnosticism, 84
Goals of Education, 48
Grant, Nigel, 211, 220
Great Britain, common syllabus, 158
Greece (legacy), 59, 70, 83, 167
Greene, Theodore Meyer, 59
Guardini, Romano, 73, 78, 91

Harris, William T., 11
Healey, Robert M., 36-39, 120
Heidegger, Martin, 74
Henry VIII, King of England, 96
Herberg, Will, 93, 179
Higgins, Msgr. George G., 128

Higher Education, religion in, 148-151, 158-159
Hill-Burton Hospital Construction Act, 29
Himmelfarb, Milton, 175, 177
Hinduism, 56, 160, 167, 168, 171-172
History, interpretation of, 74, 82, 85, 86
History, teaching of, 61
Hoefnagels, Harry, 108
Howe, Mark DeWolfe, 230
Humanism, Christian, 87
Humanism, Western, 67, 72, 78
Humanistic Education, 81
Human Nature, 79, 209

Immigration to the U.S., effect, 15; Jewish, 176
India, 170-172
Intellectualism, Christian, 83
Intolerance, 157
Islam, 56, 164, 168, 172-173

Jackson, Justice Robert H., 81, 159
Jacksonian Revolution, 128
Jacobin, 15
Jaspers, Karl, 167, 199-200
Jefferson, Thomas, 36-39, 97, 120, 150, 155, 235
Jewish attitudes toward religion in public education, 175-195; absolutism, danger of, 192, 193; alliance with Protestants and secular humanists, 184; differences in outlook between second and third generation in U.S., 179; opposition to teaching about doctrines of religions, 185; post-Jewish world, problem, 193; support of public school, 177
Jewish-Christian relations, 179
Jewish emancipation, 180, 182; self-consciousness, 179, 182, 186
Jews, 6, 16, 101, 130
John XXIII, Pope, 100, 101, 104, 111
Johnson, Lyndon, 30
Judaism, 90

Kaplan, Mordecai, 183, 186-188
Karça, Ramazan, 210
Katz, Wilbur G., 147, 232
Keppel, Francis J., 31
Kerygma, 169
Kline, George, 210
Komsomol, Russia, 212, 215, 216

Kraemer, Heinrick, 167
Khrushchev, Nikita S., 212, 225
Küng, Hans, 110-112, 168

Lackmann, Max, 104
Laicity, 233
Lambert, Bernard, 105, 189
Lamennais, H. F. R. de, 130
Landeskirche, 135
Land-grant universities, 116
Latreille (cited by Katz), 233-234
Lenin, V. I., 208, 217; attitude toward religion, 223, 225; polytechnic training, 213
Leo XIII, Pope, 131
Lerner, Max, 42, 43, 45, 47-49, 131
Liberty, religious, 91, 113; struggle for, England, 97
Lieberman, Myron, 45-46
Lincoln, Abraham, 154
Literature, teaching of, 60
Litt, Theodore, 70, 196
Lizop, Edouard, 133
Locke, John, 97
Lomonosov, Mikhail V., 225
Lutheran Church, 127

Madison, James, 129
Magic, 165
Mahoney, John F., 144-146
Makarenko, Anton Semenovich, 220-222
Mann, Horace, 11, 68
Marcel, Gabriel, 60
Maritain, Jacques, 63-66
Marty, Martin E., 23
Marx, Karl, 207, 209, 213, 223
Mass media of communication, 58
Massachusetts, nineteenth-century practice, 11
Maurer, Wilhelm, 179
McCluskey, Neil G., 11, 142-145
Mendelssohn, Moses, 181
Method, educational, 67
Methodists, 127
Michelangelo, Burnarroti, 62
Middle Ages, 87
"Milieu Christianity," 108
Miller, William, 229
Moehlman, Conrad Henry, 123
Moody, Joseph N., 10
Moral Norms, 20, 46-47, 58, 73, 79, 90, 157, 188, 198, 200, 238
Motivation (for learning), 65
Mozart, Wolfgang Amadeus, 62

Murray, John Courtney, 19, 143, 155, 193
Mystical Body, Church as, 109

Napoleon I, Emperor of France, 129-130
National Community Relations Advisory Council (Jewish), 184
National Council of Churches, 140
Natural Law, 87, 110, 121
Natural Religion, 155, 166, 168
Natural Theology, 161
Naturalism, 79, 165, 201
Nature and Grace, 84
Nazism, 68, 69, 73, 101, 104, 132, 135
New York State, refusal of parochial school subsidy, 120
Niebuhr, H. Richard, 173
Niebuhr, Reinhold, 79, 107
Nietzsche, Friedrich Wilhelm, 49
Nineteenth Century, rising interest in religion in U.S., 15
Non-Christian religions, teaching about, 164-173
Non-religious factors, 146, 164
Non-theological factors, 105
Northrop, F. S. C., 171

O'Gara, James, 141
Otto, Rudolf, 168

Paedeia, 70
Parent's Right, 31
Paul VI, Pope, 100
Persecution, religious, 157, 179
Pétain, Henri, 132
Pfeffer, Leo, 177, 184
Phenix, Philip H., 55-58
Philosophia perennis, 156
Plato, 83, 167, 201, 203
Pluralism, 13, 15, 17, 18, 22, 35, 53, 109, 123, 191, 237
Political education, post-war Germany, 76
Pollard, William G., 204
Polytechnic education, Russia, 213
Polytheism, 165
Poverty Impact Program (of Elementary and Secondary Education Act of 1965), 30
Powell, Theodore, 32
Pragmatism, 17, 40, 46, 49, 57, 63, 72, 75, 200, 238
Primitive Religion, 165
Progress, 74

Progressive education, 43-44
Prophetic religion, 94
Protestant, early, U.S., 10
Protestant cooperation, 94-95; responsibility for education, 127, 236
Protestantism, Roman Catholic view of, 112-113
Public opinion polls, 79-80, 93

Rationalism, 79
Reason, ontological and technological, 73-74
Reconstructionism, Judaism, 186
Reformation, 60, 134, 159; and the Jews, 180
Regents, New York State Board of, 5, 8
Relativism, 157, 208, 229
Religion, revival of interest in, 93
Religion, teaching about, 80, 123, 150, 153-162, 239
Religious holidays, celebration of, 16
Rerum Novarum, 131
Respect for dignity of persons, 91
Revivalism, 15, 95
Rights of Man, 90, 235
Ritual, religious, 166
Roman Catholics, 6, 16; attitudes toward public schools, pronouncements, 141-142; defensive attitude of, 140-141, 146-147; discrimination against, 139
Roman Catholic parochial schools, 95-96, 139-151; contribution of, 117; increase of enrollment, 142; Jewish opposition to tax aid, 175; problems of, 143-146
Rozenzweig, Franz, 182
Roth, Lawrence, 5
Rousseau, Jean Jacques, 72
Russell, Bertrand, 203
Russia, 40, 47, 128, 206-227; literacy, 211; modern curriculum, 211, 214; norms, "Rules for Pupils," 219; religion, attitude toward in education, 223-226; Tsarist education, 208, 211
Rutledge, Justice Wiley B., 9
Ryan, Mary Perkins, 141

Sacramentalism, 156
Schilling, Harold K., 159
Schlette, Heinz Robert, 217
Schneider, Friedrich, 71

Schubert, Franz, 62
Science (natural), 57, 59, 62, 196-205;
  conflict with religion, 197; danger
  of isolation of religion from, 204-
  205; inclusive world view, 199;
  method, 197, 204
Scientism, 168, 200, 202, 207
Sectarian conflict, 51, 57
Sectarian instruction, 154
Secular, 49, 234
Secular exclusiveness in education, 89
Secularism, 50, 61, 150, 190, 191, 234;
  positive contribution of, 191
Secularist ideology, 82
Secularist pressure, 13-14, 16, 18
Secularization, 49
Separation of Church and State, 12,
  14, 19, 116, 119, 121, 122, 139, 143,
  148
Seward, William, Governor of New
  York State, 120
Shared Time, 31-33, 148
Shinto, 171
Shuster, George, 159
Siegel, Samuel, 190-194
Social change, cultural implications,
  58; new conditions, 23; nineteenth-
  century patterns of piety, 235
Socrates, 83, 167, 201
Space exploration, 197-198
Standards, educational, 44-45
Stearns, Harry L., 31
Stewart, Justice Potter, 27
Stoicism, 84
Sunday School, 95, 120
Supreme Court Decisions, 3-10, 13,
  25-30; Abington v. Schempp and
  Murray v. Curlett (Bible-Reading
  and Lord's Prayer Decision), 4, 8;
  Cochran v. Louisiana (textbook),
  32, 34; Engel v. Vitale (Regents'
  Prayer Decision), 3-7, 29, 148; Ever-
  son v. Board of Education (school
  bus), 8, 9, 25, 32; McCollum v.
  Board of Education (released time),

9, 25-27, 33, 148; Zorach v. Clauson
  (released time), 7, 9, 27-28, 35
Symbolism, religious, 78
Synagogue Council of America, 184

Taoism, 170
Tax exemption for religious agencies,
  28
Teacher education, 53, 160
Teacher shortage, 96
Technology, 60, 74, 202, 230
Theonomous Culture, 86
Tillich, Paul, 55-56, 59, 73, 86
Thomism, 167
Tolerance, 97, 157, 171
Tolstoi, Count Leo, 208
Totalitarianism, 46, 59, 63
Toynbee, Arnold J., 81, 164, 172
Truth, 66, 70, 73, 74, 90

Ulich, Robert, 49
Ultimacy, 55-56
United States, expansion across con-
  tinent and growth of educational
  system, 131
Universities, see Higher Education

Values, lack of in nihilism, 237
Vatican Council, Second, 98, 100, 102,
  104-113
Vialatoux (cited by Katz), 232-233
Voluntarism, 128, 230, 231

Wall of separation between Church
  and State, 8, 28, 36; criticism of
  phrase by Clancy, 231
Wars of religion, 100
Weimar Republic, 134
Welter, Rush, 89-90, 128
Whitehead, Alfred North, 203-204
World Council of Churches, 99-100

Young Pioneers, Russia, 215

Zionism, 182